Babes and Brides

Two One-Act Plays

by Eric Berlin

GW00643261

SAMUEL FRENCH, INC.
45 West 25th Street   NEW YORK 10010
7623 Sunset Boulevard HOLLYWOOD 90046
LONDON   TORONTO

"You don't feel you can love me,
but I feel you could."

— Paul Simon
"Gumboots"

IMPORTANT BILLING AND CREDIT REQUIREMENTS

All producers of THE LINE THAT PICKED UP 1000 BABES (and how it can work for you!) and/or THE MIDNIGHT MOONLIGHT WEDDING CHAPEL must give credit to the Author of the Play(s) in all programs distributed in connection with performances of the Play(s) and in all instances in which the title(s) of the Play appear(s) for purposes of advertising, publicizing or otherwise exploiting the Play(s) and/or a production. The name of the Author *must* also appear on a separate line, on which no other name appears, immediately following the title, and *must* appear in size of type not less than fifty percent the size of the title type.

The Line That's Picked Up 1000 Babes (and how it can work for you!)

The Line That's Picked Up 1000 Babes (and how it can work for you!) made its New York City premiere at The Spot! at Café Arielle on June 5th 1992, directed by Susan L. Hitzmann, and had the following cast:

ALAN	Thomas Shillue
BENNY	John Di Domenico
ELLEN	Julie Bowen
FRAN	Virginia Smith
DIANE	Ivi Brenner
CHARLIE	Rupert Ravens

This play is dedicated to John Nagle,
Chris Ries, Stephen Guirgis,
Tara Davidoff, Sonia Zizilas,
Marion Schwartz, and
Bill Braine

CHARACTERS

ALAN

BENNY

ELLEN

FRAN

DIANE

CHARLIE

TIME & PLACE

Friday night.
A singles bar.

Scene 1
The Line That's Picked Up 1000 Babes
Part I

ALAN. This place is a goddamn meat market.

BENNY. People meet people, that's all.

ALAN. That's all.

BENNY. They have to. You're here, too, don't forget.

ALAN. I'm here being me.

BENNY. What's that mean?

ALAN. Being *me*. You're here being whoever happens to be popular at the time. What that *book* says.

BENNY. Man, forget the book, can't you?

ALAN. No. I can't. It's too stupid to just forget.

BENNY. Well, try. (Man.)

ALAN. I have a couple of questions.

BENNY. About the book?

ALAN. Yes. Okay? Then I'll back off.

BENNY. Bullshit.

ALAN. Just listen.

BENNY. What.

ALAN. Okay. Question Number One. If there's *one line* that's picked up a thousand babes, like it says, then why is that book two hundred pages long?

BENNY. Well, hell. What you don't know. There's more to it than just the line. There's

more. You have to say it the right way. There's a
way to say the line ... You have to say it to the right
girl. You—

ALAN. The right girl?

BENNY. Yes.

ALAN. Okay. *(Pause. ALAN stifles a grin.)*
No, go on, what?

BENNY. What's the matter with that? Stop
putting down what you don't know about, huh? You
can't say the line to just anybody. You can't try to
pick up some ninety-year-old lady.

ALAN. Is that what the book said or did you
figure that out by yourself?

BENNY. There's a long chapter as to who the
right girl is.

ALAN. You mean "babe."

BENNY. Yeah, girl, babe, whatever.

ALAN. Which leads me to my second
question. I've always wanted to ask this. What the
hell is a "babe"?

BENNY. A girl, you moron.

ALAN. You see? When was that book written?
Nobody calls girls "babes" anymore.

BENNY. Oh no?

ALAN. *Do* they?

BENNY. You don't call them babes to their
faces. Unless you're trying to make some *point*—

ALAN. Oh! Behind their *backs*! I get it.

BENNY. Alan: It's just the same thing. Babes
are girls. The guidelines in this book—

ALAN. Are time-tested, I know, you told me.

BENNY. It was written in the seventies. Babes then are girls now.

ALAN. But not every girl is a babe.

BENNY. No.

ALAN. The book says that.

BENNY. Right.

ALAN. A very specific type of girl. Less than ninety, for one thing.

BENNY. Yes.

ALAN. Say, eighty-six, eighty-seven ...

BENNY. Now, look—

ALAN. So where do you draw the line? Are there forty-year-old babes out there?

BENNY. Don't use the book, okay? Don't even listen to me. All right? But what I'm saying: This book has been time-tested. It works.

ALAN. Actually, I hear that some girls don't even like to be called *girls* now. They're *women*.

BENNY. That is the worst kind of girl.

ALAN. You mean, girls who think. Girls who think are automatically out.

BENNY. They can think, I don't care.

ALAN. They just can't think *a lot*. Does that book give you tips on how to talk about current events?

BENNY. Current events? Who talks about current events in a bar like this?

ALAN. How'd the authors of that book know you'd be *coming* to a bar like this?

BENNY. They said to.

ALAN. Which brings me to my third question: Why would you take a handbook for picking up girls to the bar you plan on patronizing? Wouldn't it be a better idea to just read it and leave it home? You don't want the girls here to *know* you're using a book, now, do you?

BENNY. I have it in my coat pocket. It's a pocket-sized book. They'll never know I have it. If I have to read it, I'll go into the men's room.

ALAN. What if it falls out? You're having a drink with this girl—this *babe*—and you've used the great "line" and a couple of pretty good back-up lines, and then she tells a really funny joke. And you laugh so hard that you almost fall over backwards, but you get your balance back, but out of your coat pocket falls this *book*. Naturally it falls face up, so the title is readable by everyone in the room, so everyone knows that you're using a handbook to pick up girls. And once they know that, no girl on the planet will ever speak to you again.

BENNY. That won't happen.

ALAN. Why's that, babes can't tell jokes, either?

BENNY. I mean the book won't fall out.

ALAN. Oooookay. Now. About this *babe* business. Show me a babe.

BENNY. Let's see ... her. Over there.

ALAN. Where?

BENNY. By the jukebox.

ALAN. Looking in at it?

BENNY. Yeah.

ALAN. How can you tell? She's not even facing this direction. You don't even know what she looks like.

BENNY. You don't need to know what she looks like.

ALAN. Then what the hell are you going by?

BENNY. Look at the way she's dressed. Tight blue jeans is the first thing talked about in Chapter Three.

ALAN. Chapter Three?

BENNY. Chapter Three: "What is a Babe?"

ALAN. There—*wait*. There she is. Okay, now you see what she looks like. Is she a babe?

BENNY. Yes. Definitely.

ALAN. Why? What seals it?

BENNY. The make-up.

ALAN. She's wearing too much. I see her face and I *still* don't know what she looks like.

BENNY. That's just it. Too much make-up is a sure sign.

ALAN. A sure sign. Of ... babeness.

BENNY. Call them what you will.

ALAN. But, now, wait, do you *like* girls with too much make-up?

BENNY. I can take them or leave them.

ALAN. Or take them and then leave them.

BENNY. Now that's not fair.

ALAN. Okay, sorry ... so are you going to do something about her?

BENNY. I don't know, maybe. Maybe.

Scene 2
Happy Birthday

ELLEN. You look so *glum*, already. I said I'm sorry. Really.

FRAN. I'm not upset, okay? Just stop.

ELLEN. I forgot your birthday.

FRAN. So. So what? It's no crime. And it's no big deal.

ELLEN. Well, happy birthday anyway.

FRAN. Thanks again.

ELLEN. And I'm sorry.

FRAN. There's nothing to be sorry for.

ELLEN. I *knew* it last week. It buzzed through my mind. And then I forgot until just today.

FRAN. It's okay.

ELLEN. I was at work, standing over the photocopying machine, and it hit me, *Oh my God!,* it's your birthday. And I made a note to get you a card on the way home ...

FRAN. But you forgot. It's *okay.* It's no big deal.

ELLEN. But what happened was, Eddie, that guy at work with the blue eyes who I was seeing for a while but then he dropped me for whatzername, the one who always wears these short short skirts even in winter? *He* comes by and wants to know if I want to go out sometime, and I said, "Out for *what*?" and he said not to be like that, that he had made a mistake and that we should go out and try to start over. He wants to take things slowly. He doesn't want to go as fast. I always wonder where guys think the speedometer is on these relationships. So I said I'd think about it, and he said he'd call me, and you know, I think I'm going to go out with him again. Why not? I mean, if he wants to take things slowly then there's nothing to worry about, right?

FRAN. I guess.

ELLEN. So when that all happened, I forgot ... I'm sorry.

FRAN. It's okay. Just forget about it.

ELLEN. You need to learn how to drop hints better. When my birthday is coming, I take out advertising in the newspaper.

FRAN. I don't want to have to remind people.

ELLEN. It's better than having them forget.

FRAN. It doesn't matter.

ELLEN. Don't be a martyr. You deserve to be upset. I'd kill you if you forgot mine. *(Pause.)* If you're going to be upset, *be upset.*

FRAN. *I don't WANT to be upset.* OKAY?

ELLEN. Okay, okay. I really am sorry. But, look, I'm taking you out right? Here we are.

FRAN. Yeah. Here we are. Your favorite bar.

ELLEN. You wanted to come here.

FRAN. No. I didn't.

ELLEN. Then why'd you come when I asked?

FRAN. When you *asked*? *You* didn't *ask.* You practically put a leash on me and dragged me here.

ELLEN. What's the matter with this place?

FRAN. Nothing ...

ELLEN. What? What is it?

FRAN. I don't like standing around here watching guys try to pick you up.

ELLEN. Oh come on.

FRAN. Don't start.

ELLEN. You act as if I get all this *attention*.

FRAN. You do!

ELLEN. You act as if you get *none*.

FRAN. I *don't*.

ELLEN. They try to pick you up too, don't give me that.

FRAN. They pick me up and move me out of the way so they can get to you.

ELLEN. Oh come *on*.

FRAN. It's true and you know it. Why else *would* this be your favorite bar?

ELLEN. ... it has good drinks.

FRAN. Whaaat?

ELLEN. It *does*.

FRAN. All you drink is beer. You can get the same beer in Shop-Rite.

ELLEN. Well, that's my favorite supermarket.

FRAN. Can't we just go? We've been here long enough.

ELLEN. Hey. See? Look. That guy's looking at you.

FRAN. Oh, sorry. I must be blocking his view of you.

ELLEN. No, *look*. See?

FRAN. ... how can you possibly tell what he's looking at? This bar is so dark, I can't even see you.

ELLEN. He *is,* I swear.

FRAN. I hope you're someone I know.

ELLEN. You can tell what people are looking at with a little practice.

FRAN. Okay, so he's looking in this *direction.* He's got to be looking somewhere.

ELLEN. And he's choosing to look at you.... he's kinda cute ...

FRAN. How can you *tell? You* can't tell what he looks like from here ...

ELLEN. So go over there and see for yourself.

FRAN. I don't want to go over there. I didn't want to come into the bar in the first place, I certainly don't want to go exploring it.

ELLEN. Fine, fine.

FRAN. So can we go please? Let that be my birthday present.

ELLEN. I bet he comes over here. He's *definitely* looking, kiddo.

FRAN. Guy must have eyes like a fucking hawk.

ELLEN. Just stay until he comes over here.

FRAN. How do you know he will.

ELLEN. Trust me.

FRAN. Oh, Jesus.

ELLEN. I just want to show you that you get more attention than you think you do.

FRAN. I don't want that proved to me.

ELLEN. I'm going to give you your birthday present. Self-esteem.

FRAN. This is terrible! Listen to yourself! I'm going to have self-esteem if some sleazy guy in a bar tries to pick me up? You'll have to excuse me, but I don't make the connection!

ELLEN. You know what it means when a guy picks you up?

FRAN. *Tries* to.

ELLEN. Tries to?

FRAN. What.

ELLEN. You see, guys are real self-conscious. So there has to be a real motivating force if they're going to attempt a discourse with a member of the opposite sex. Exterior beauty is the most obvious exterior force. There's no doubt you've got a great personality, but it is the *exterior attractiveness* that's going to get the key in the lock—

FRAN. So to speak.

ELLEN. —so when strangers start talking to you in bars, it's a compliment, see?

FRAN. Psychology majors should be shot upon graduation.

ELLEN. You disagree?

FRAN. I agree, I agree. I didn't understand anything you said, but if it makes you happy, I'll agree.

ELLEN. Do you *dis*agree?

FRAN. I just said I agree.

ELLEN. Okay ...

FRAN. Now can we go?

ELLEN. No! How are you going to know otherwise?

FRAN. Know what??

ELLEN. What he thinks of you?

FRAN. I don't *care* what he thinks of me! Who the hell is *he*? We're standing in the same building so that means he's allowed to pass judgment on whether I'm a part of the human race or not?

ELLEN. So fine, sit there and be lonely.

FRAN. I'm not lonely. I'm *alone*.

ELLEN. *Fran*. They're the same thing.

Scene 3
Hello, She Said

DIANE. *(Brightly.)* Hello.

CHARLIE. Oh yeah, HI! How're you doing?

DIANE. Okay, what about you?

CHARLIE. Doing good, doing good. I've never been here before, quite a place. I'm running into every single person I've ever known in my entire life. You ever have a day like that?

DIANE. Yeah ...

CHARLIE. They say if you stand in one place long enough you'll run into every person you know. But, hell, I thought it'd take longer than a couple of hours.

DIANE. Uh-huh—

CHARLIE. And I thought they were talking about, you know, Penn Station or something. Disneyworld. A place people GO to. Who comes here? No one. But I guess I'm wrong, because I'm running into every SINGLE person I've *ever known*.

DIANE. It's a small world.

CHARLIE. It's a *very* small world. *Very* small. I ran into some girl before, she comes up to me like we're the oldest of friends. Her name's Joan, Jane, John, something like that. You know who she turns out to be? She's my ... wait, wait, I want to get this straight. She's my ex-girlfriend's sister's friend's *older brother's* ex-girlfriend. Is that stretching it or what? And here I am talking to her like I may have at one time saved her life. "Hi, how you doing, been a long time, yeah." I can't believe I recognized her. What, did I see her *once,* maybe twice? Maybe said five words to her. And two of them were "Gesundheit." And the damn thing is, it happens all the time. Makes me feel like I'm losing my mind sometime. I pass people out on the street, they say hello to me, I say hello to them, I walk away saying, who the fuck was that? It gets to the point that I say hello to every person I make eye contact with. I mean, I don't want to seem unfriendly, so instead I seem homosexual. No, no, that's not true, sorry. I'm getting drunk. When I get drunk, I babble. I don't know why I babble when I get drunk, it's just something I do, I babble. My friends all say "You *babble* when you get drunk," and they're right, it's something I do, I babble. Because I don't care too much when it's a guy says hello to me and I don't know who he is. I mean, it bothers me a little, but I'm not going to spend the day agonizing over it.

But the *girls,* I get these pretty girls who are just so happy to see me, and I'm happy to see them too, and I'd be even happier if I *knew who they fucking were*! But, you know, you can't *ask,* right? You can't tell some girl you don't know who she is, she'll be insulted. Right? Right?

DIANE. I don't know ...

CHARLIE. See, I'll prove it, who the fuck are you?

DIANE. Wha—

CHARLIE. See, you're insulted, right?

DIANE. Well, it's the way you *ask.*

CHARLIE. Everybody wants to be remembered but no one does anything memorable.

DIANE. You really don't know me, or is this an experiment?

CHARLIE. I *really* don't know you. I haven't known a single person I've spoken to all night. I want to get just one name. One name. So who *are you already*?

DIANE. Guess.

CHARLIE. AWWWW, NO NO NO NO NO, don't make me guess.

DIANE. Give it a shot.

CHARLIE. Do you know how many ways I know people? We've got this *humongous* office I work in, it's like the population of Calcutta in one building. We've got these night classes I'm taking. We've got the apartment building I live in, twenty floors of the friendliest strangers in the world. I say hello to all of them, I don't know a single solitary name. I know all the *dogs'*

names... I don't *know* who you are, I'm not
kidding. What, it's not like I *slept* with you or
anything ...

DIANE. Yes.

CHARLIE. *YES?* What yes?

DIANE. You asked me a question.

CHARLIE. That wasn't a real question. I
didn't ... I ... *(Pause.)* What was that, "Yes, I slept
with you?" Or "Yes, I *didn't* sleep with you?"

DIANE. Guess.

CHARLIE. What is this? What are you, testing
my psychic ability? I *slept* with you? *(THEY stare
at each other.)* Nawwww. I couldn't have. I
couldn't have, have, have slept with you. Maybe
taken a *nap* or something, but ... all night?

DIANE. Dusk 'til dawn.

CHARLIE. When?

DIANE. Last mon—two months ago.

CHARLIE. Two months ago. You're telling me
that I met you, and we ...

DIANE. It was wonderful.

CHARLIE. And we met ... uh ...

DIANE. You *still* don't know? That *party* ... ?

CHARLIE. Good Jesus. *(HE looks at her.)* Oh.
Ohhhh, yeah! I remember you now! My God. You
know, I've had a lot on my mind lately. Work
and everything. It's interfering with my life. I'm
going to be senile by the time I'm thirty. I'm lucky
I can find way home at night sometimes. Yeah,
yeah, I'm sorry, I remember you now, of course.
How *are* you?

DIANE. I'm doing just fine.

CHARLIE. Good, good to hear. I'm fine too. Look, I have to go now, but it was *really GREAT* seeing you again. We should get together some time, give me a call, huh?

DIANE. So what's my name?

CHARLIE. Huh?

DIANE. My name. Do you remember me? What's my name?

CHARLIE. Why, it's, uh ... SHIT SHIT SHIT, I don't *know*. I'm so embarrassed, this is the worst thing— I ... I mean ... You ... ARrrrgggh ... I feel so callous. I swear, I must have been really really drunk when we met, because I don't remember anything. I don't usually *do* that, but I'm sorry if I did. I'm sorry I don't remember you. I'm not the biggest ladies man in the world, so when I actually ... I mean, I usually *remember* that it happened! I feel so *bad,* I mean ... ugh. I really did ... this?

DIANE. Ummm, no.

CHARLIE. Whaaat?

DIANE. No, you didn't.

CHARLIE. I didn't?

DIANE. I was just kidding.

CHARLIE. Just ...

DIANE. I'm really sorry. I'm a little embarrassed.

CHARLIE. You were kidding? So then we ... I mean, you and me, we ...

DIANE. No. Nothing.

CHARLIE. Oh thank GOD!

DIANE. *I beg* your pardon?

CHARLIE. I mean, no offense, I just though—

DIANE. No, no, don't worry about it.

CHARLIE. So, if we *didn't* ... uh, then how do I know you?

DIANE. What?

CHARLIE. How do I *know* you?

DIANE. Oh, that.

CHARLIE. Yeah. I mean, we do know each other, right? ...*right?*

DIANE. Ummmm, don't kill me, okay?

CHARLIE. I'm not guaranteeing anything.

DIANE. Ohh ... well, you don't know me.

CHARLIE. I don't know you.

DIANE. I've never seen you before in my life. You *look* like someone I know, though. Really.

CHARLIE. Is that why you said hello?

DIANE. Yeah ... we made, you know, "eye contact," I thought you might be someone I knew, so I said Hi. If I know you, I don't know why either.

CHARLIE. I think this might be funny.

DIANE. It is. Really. And if it isn't, then we'll just never see each other again anyway, right? Probably.

CHARLIE. Probably we will. Small world, remember.

DIANE. Yeah, well ...

CHARLIE. If I do see you, though ...

DIANE. Yeah?

CHARLIE. I'm not saying hello.

Scene 4
Beesh Bosh Bish

ELLEN. Well, *hi*, Benny. Ellen. And this is Fran.

BENNY. Hi. Hi.

ELLEN. *Fran* here is an up-and-coming musician. Isn't that right?

BENNY. That right? ... err, what do you play?

FRAN. Th—

ELLEN. I can't play an instrument to save my life, myself

BENNY. What do *you* do?

ELLEN. I'm a secretary.

BENNY. That right.

ELLEN. I didn't mean to be a secretary, I mean, I've got a degree in psychology and all that ... but, what the heck. I was born knowing how to type. ... but I can't play an instrument here, like Fran. She's really good.

FRAN. It's just a matter of practice.

BENNY. What do you play?

ELLEN. She plays the flute.

FRAN. I—yeah.

ELLEN. She's good. You should hear her sometime. I took piano lessons once. I took six years of piano lessons and all I can tell you is where Middle C is. Give or take. Just no talent, what can I say.

BENNY. My mom made me take piano lessons, too. And the violin. And the trumpet.

ELLEN. Don't you hate that? And then they yell at you because you're not practicing each and every instrument they force you to play.

BENNY. Well, no. I didn't take them all at the sa—

ELLEN. I know *exactly* what you mean.

BENNY. Bu—

ELLEN. *My* mom made me take ballet, tap and modern dance at the age of nine. I made them all look the same. They *all* looked modern. They looked *new wave.* My mom would say "Why don't you practice your ballet now?" "I *am* practicing, Ma!" See, I liked my tap shoes, I liked the noise they made. So I wore them even when I was doing ballet. When I did a pirouette, I made a hole in the floor. *(Pause.)* Anyway, I don't think Fran ever took any dancing lessons, did you, Fran?

FRAN. Yeah. Right. No.

(Pause.)

ELLEN. But she's really good at the flute.

BENNY. So I hear.

ELLEN. C'mon, Fran, tell him about the flute!

FRAN. Tell him? Well, uh ... it's this long silver rod with holes in it and what you do is you *blow*—

ELLEN. Fran! Come on! She's kidding. She gets like this. It's her birthday.

BENNY. Yeah? Happy birthday.

FRAN. Thanks.

ELLEN. I'm taking her out for her birthday.

BENNY. To where?

ELLEN. To *here*.

BENNY. Oh.

FRAN. But we have to leave soon.

ELLEN. No we don't.

FRAN. Yes we *d*—

ELLEN. I'm taking her out because I forgot to get her a card. I was reminding myself all day today but then at the office, this guy who I used to go out with came over to me and we started talking an—

FRAN. Excuse me, excuse me? Hello? *(To Benny.)* Can I ask you a question?

BENNY. Uh, yeah. Sure.

FRAN. It's kind of personal.

BENNY. Ookay ...

FRAN. Be honest.

BENNY. All right.

FRAN. Which one of us did you come over to pick up?

BENNY. Sorry?

ELLEN. *FRAN!*

FRAN. No, really, I want to know. 'Cause it's kind of silly for the person that you're *not* picking up to even stick around, right? So if you're trying to pick *her* up, I'm going to go find an all-night bookstore or something, okay? To keep me occupied, all right?

BENNY. I ... I ...

ELLEN. Just ignore her. She's just cranky because it's her birthday. She hates birthdays.

FRAN. I don't hate birthdays when people remember them!

ELLEN. I said I'm fucking sorry, what do you want me to do, melt into the floor?

FRAN. I just want to get out of here.

ELLEN. You hate this bar *that much*?

FRAN. YES! *(Calling out.)* I hate this bar! How many times do I have to say it?

ELLEN. You wouldn't even give it a chance.

FRAN. A chance to what? Turn into an Italian restaurant?

ELLEN. You want to go, fine then, *fine*!

FRAN. Thank goodness, let's get out of here.

ELLEN. Can I finish my drink first?

FRAN. I'll get you a straw.

BENNY. Uhhh ... will you excuse me? I, uh, have to go to the bathroom. *(HE leaves. As HE exits, HE pulls his manual from his pocket and runs offstage trying to find his place in the book.)*

ELLEN. I can't believe you *said* that to him.

FRAN. Why?

ELLEN. You don't say things like that to people!

FRAN. *Why?* People come here to pick up other people. That's what you tell me. So, now, what? What are you, pretending that's not true?

ELLEN. You embarrassed him. Poor guy. He liked you, too.

FRAN. WHAT? How the fuck could you *tell*? YOU were doing all the talking.

ELLEN. I was talking about you. I was talking about the flute.

FRAN. You were talking about pianos! You were talking about your office!

ELLEN. I was not.

FRAN. How can you say that! Of *course* you were!

ELLEN. Well, I had to talk about myself a little, I mean, come on.

FRAN. A little? You gave him your life story. I thought you were going to bring out a photo album.

(CHARLIE enters the scene.)

ELLEN. I w— wait a minute, wait a minute ... excuse me!

FRAN. Holy *shit*!

ELLEN. *(To Charlie.)* Hello?

CHARLIE. *(Ominously.)* Hello.

ELLEN. Don't I know you from somewhere?

CHARLIE. I would never deny it.

ELLEN. I thought so!

FRAN. You want to hurry up with that drink, already?

ELLEN. Oh, come on ... it's not like we're in a *rush* ... *(To Charlie.)* So where do I know you from?

CHARLIE. I have no idea. I've been seeing these people all night who I don't know *who* they fucking ... — wait a minute. OH MY GOD! I *DO* KNOW YOU!!

ELLEN. Well, yes, that's what I just said.

CHARLIE. You work in my office! You're Roger's secretary! *I know who you ARE!!*

ELLEN. ... well, I'm happy to see you, too.

CHARLIE. No, no, it's not that I'm happy to *see* you ...

ELLEN. What?

CHARLIE. I mean ... no, wait. Let me try that again. Yes, I'm happy to see you. I'm really, yes, yes, I'm happy. I'm just glad, you know, that, that I *know* you. At all. I've been seeing these people all night who ... they ... Never mind, it's really a long story.

ELLEN. You're drunk, aren't you?

CHARLIE. DING! Point for the blonde. Want to buy a vowel?

ELLEN. So what are you doing here?

CHARLIE. You just *SAID*. Getting *DRUNK*

FRAN. Shhhhhhh.

CHARLIE. *Am I talking too loud??* I'm sorry, that always happens. I mean, it always happens when I drink. My friends say "You talk so *loud* when you get drunk." So I'm drinking and it's happening. See. I'll whisper now, okay? Shhhhh...

FRAN. You also talk a lot when you're drunk.

CHARLIE. Yes, but at least now I'm talking a lot *softly*.

ELLEN. Well, my name's Ellen.

CHARLIE. Really?

ELLEN. Yes, really.

CHARLIE. Oh. (*HE nods his head, as if in deep understanding*)

ELLEN. (*After a confused pause*) And, uh, this is Fran.

CHARLIE. Hi.
FRAN. Well, hi.

(Pause.)

ELLEN. What is your name?
CHARLIE. Oh, you don't know that, do you? As a matter of fact, that's why you said *your* name, isn't it?
FRAN. You're getting the sharp ones tonight, Ellen.
CHARLIE. Pardon me. My name's Charlie. Hi.
FRAN. Hi.

(Pause.)

ELLEN. *Fran* here is an up-and-coming mumphph— *(FRAN has elbowed Ellen.)*
CHARLIE. What?
ELLEN. Uh ... I'm a secretary, what do you do?
CHARLIE. I already know what you do. You work in my office.
ELLEN. Oh yeah! I forgot. HA! .... So what else do you do?
CHARLIE. What else do I do? What do you mean?
ELLEN. I mean, outside of work. For instance, Fran here plays the flute.

(FRAN bangs down her glass, then smiles at Charlie.)

CHARLIE. The flute, that's nice.

FRAN. Thank you.

CHARLIE. I always wanted to take an instrument. Do something creative. Ballet.

FRAN. Ballet??

CHARLIE. Well, not *ballet,* per se. It's the first creative thing that popped into my head.

ELLEN. I took ballet.

FRAN. I was about to say, you don't look like your typical ballerina. Or whatever male ballerinas are called.

CHARLIE. Uhh ... ballerinos.

FRAN. Yeah, that must be it.

ELLEN. I took ballet, too. And tap. I took them at the same time. I used to wear my tap shoes even when I practiced ballet ... isn't that funny?

CHARLIE. You took ballet, "too?" Who was the first person?

ELLEN. Well, uh, you were.

CHARLIE. Huh ...? ME?? Took *ballet? (Begins to laugh.)* Oh God! I, ... can you see me in a ... *(HE is drunk and uncontrollably laughing. And laughter, which is contagious, catches to FRAN.)* Can you see me in a pair of lavender tights? And a tu-tu? *(Improvises some quick ballet moves, humming "The Nutcracker.")* La-la-la-la-la-la ... No, no ... *(Calms down somewhat.)* I don't think so. I have all the grace of a dead fish.

ELLEN. I didn't think it was that funny.

CHARLIE. *(Snorts, trying to keep control.)* Yeah. It was. Okay, I'm better. All right. All right. I was in Bermuda, but I'm back now.

(Silence, then FRAN hums The Nutcracker again. FRAN and CHARLIE crack up again while ELLEN just stares at them.)

FRAN. What is the matter with me? I'm not even *drunk*! Okay. Okay. This isn't that funny.

CHARLIE. Okay, okay, let's just ... let's just calm down. I'm going to need oxygen in a minute.

BENNY. *(Returns.)* Hey, what's going on here, what'd I miss? Who's this guy?

CHARLIE. "This guy?" Me?

BENNY. Yeah.

ELLEN. He works with me in my office.

CHARLIE. But I'm a ballet dancer on the side.

FRAN. *(To Charlie.)* Which side?

CHARLIE. The left side.

FRAN. Ah.

BENNY. Looks drunk to me.

ELLEN. He is.

CHARLIE. YOU are a very perceptive young man, sir.

BENNY. *(Sourly.)* Yeah, okay.

CHARLIE. Is it me or did the temperature of this bar just go down like thirty degrees?

FRAN. They probably turned down the heat. It's a very cheap bar, in case you haven't noticed from the dazzling light show.

ELLEN. What do you want, a *Saturday Night Fever* dance floor?

FRAN. How about light to read by?

BENNY. Read what?

FRAN. *I* don't know. The ... the beer labels.

CHARLIE. Your palm.

FRAN. The bumps on my head.

CHARLIE. How can you read the bumps on your own head?

FRAN. That's a good point.

BENNY. *(To Ellen.)* Are they both drunk?

ELLEN. *He* is. I don't know what *her* problem is. He just came over and started talking.

FRAN. *(To Benny.)* Yeah, right. Not like you did. See, *he* came over and started *talking*. You came over and started *talking*. Two very, very different things. You see?

BENNY. Nnn ... *what?*

ELLEN. Oh, ignore her, I told you she's in one of her moods.

BENNY. *(Aside, to Ellen.)* Is this guy bothering you, or what? You seem ...

ELLEN. Naw ... no. Don't worry.

BENNY. You're sure now? I can't stand people who don't know when to quit drinking.

ELLEN. He's ... he's ...

BENNY. Hey, you, drunk guy. Maybe you should just let the two of them alone, huh?

CHARLIE. What?

BENNY. I said—

CHARLIE. Who are *you?*

BENNY. Just a friend of hers. You're drunk.

CHARLIE. You keep pointing that out to me. I *know* I'm drunk. I drank the liquor that got me like this.

BENNY. Well, you're bothering my friend here.

ELLEN. No, really—

FRAN. *Bothering?* Who in th—

BENNY. Don't worry, don't worry.

FRAN. Who do you think—

CHARLIE. What is this? Ohhhhhhhh, I see.

BENNY. See what? Come on.

FRAN. *Cut it—*

ELLEN. There really isn't any need t—

CHARLIE. What I *see*—

ELLEN. All right, *all right!* HEY!

CHARLIE. I see a guy who's trying to impress some girl who so far hasn't been drooling over his winning ways. "Get rid of the drunk guy, that'll show them I'm tough."

FRAN. Hey! Hey, guys! Stop fighting over us, huh? You guys are not coyote. *We* are not dead antelope. Okay?

(Pause.)

BENNY. All right, all right, forget it.

CHARLIE. Just because I'm stupid doesn't mean I'm drunk.

BENNY. *(With a look towards Ellen.)* Yeah, right, okay.

CHARLIE. Really. What would you like to have a conversation about? Politics? Current events?

BENNY. What is this? Who talks about current events in a bar like this?

FRAN. Literature.

CHARLIE. Literature!

ELLEN. Music! You know what album I just bought?

CHARLIE. Literature! Hey, what book you reading?

BENNY. What?

CHARLIE. You have a book there, what book is that? Let me see?

BENNY. Get the hell out of here!

CHARLIE. What do you think, I wouldn't have heard of it? Come on, what book is it?

BENNY. There's no book, get away!

CHARLIE. What no book! What's that?

BENNY. Get— Get outta, HEY!

(THEY are grappling, CHARLIE trying to reach into Benny's jacket pocket for the book.)

ELLEN. *(Over the scuffle)* The Beatles! You know, I didn't even know how many songs they sang! That Happy Birthday song? That's them! You, you *guys*! Don't— ohh! STOP FIGHTING, come on!

(The book drops on to the floor. CHARLIE and BENNY scramble for it. CHARLIE wins.)

BENNY. *Give* that—!

(Pause.)

CHARLIE. "The Line That's Picked Up 1000 Babes...?" I was wrong, you must be more well-read than I am, because ... *(Starts to laugh.)* because I've never heard of this!

FRAN. The Line That's Picked Up 1000 Babes?

CHARLIE. "And How It Can Work For You!" How could I not have read it! Obviously a classic in its field!

BENNY. GIVE that—!! *(HE grabs it.)*

CHARLIE. Hey, hey, where's the chapter on how to throw drunk guys out of bars to impress the *babe* you're picking up?

BENNY. Well. I. I'm sorry. *(HE leaves.)*

CHARLIE. Sure! Suddenly he's not the hottest shit on the block anymore! Imagine that!

ELLEN. You *asshole*!

CHARLIE. Yeah! *(Beat.)* Wait, ME??? What'd *I* do?

ELLEN. What'd he do to you? God, you made him feel like shit!

CHARLIE. Are you *crazy*? Listen to me: he was trying to pick you up using a guidebook. (I don't even believe it.) He had that book *with him*! He wasn't using it for hints, it was his Bible! His *cookbook,* and you were his recipe. Chicken Ellenzinni! You *like* that? You have even a glimmer of respect for that? You're nuttier than *he* is!

ELLEN. That doesn't mean you can treat him like shit!

CHARLIE. What *is* this? You're nuttier sober than I am *drunk*!

FRAN. You don't ha—

CHARLIE. *(To Fran.)* See you later. It was nice being a drunk person near you. *(HE leaves.)*

(Pause.)

FRAN. Well. You sure know how to attract guys.

ELLEN. He was an idiot.

FRAN. First of all, I don't know how you can tell that in only five minutes. *Secondly,* if he *was* an idiot, at least he was a idiot with a personality. Unlike *your* hero.

ELLEN. He was a nice guy!

FRAN. "The Line That's Picked Up 1000 Babes?" Are you serious? BABES?

ELLEN. You've never heard the word "babe" before, is that what you want me to believe?

FRAN. Oh, I've heard it. I've always felt, though, that "babes" should be beaten to death with a croquet mallet.

ELLEN. It's common English. Get used to it.

FRAN. I don't want to. I don't want to have to get used to words like "babe." I don't want to have to deal with guys who have to use fucking *handbooks* because they're too stupid to talk by themselves. Therefore, I don't want to be in this bar anymore. I never wanted to come here. But you're so goddamn selfish, you couldn't see that.

ELLEN. Oh, now I'm selfish.

FRAN. Oh, it didn't start just now, believe me.

ELLEN. You've got a bad point or two yourself, kid.

FRAN. I'm sure I do. But at least I don't talk about myself *so* constantly, *so* regularly, that no one else can get a word in unless they fucking KILL YOU.

ELLEN. I'm sorry I forgot your damn birthday, awright!

FRAN. THIS HAS NOTHING TO DO WITH MY BIRTHDAY!

ELLEN. Oh, come on, admit it, this has everything to do with your birthday. You're mad that everyone forgot, but you never told anybody when it was! What are we supposed to do, read your mind? YOU are an indirect communicator!

FRAN. You use one more psychological term in this conversation, you are gonna *get it*—

ELLEN. Let me tell you then: you never say what you want, and then you're disappointed when you don't get it. And then you make those of us who didn't give it to you feel guilty, for no good reason. Speak *up* for chrissakes!

FRAN. Speak up? And be *you*? You're about as subtle as a bulldozer; is that what you recommend for me? You told me you were setting that guy—Benny—up for me, but when he came over here, you threw yourself at his feet!

ELLEN. You said you didn't like him!

FRAN. Wait, wait, this gets better! And then came Charlie, who actually seemed cool, but he really *was* looking at me, so you drove him off! 'Cause you wanted to be the center of attention!

ELLEN. I didn't drive him off!

FRAN. You did so! You called him an asshole!

ELLEN. He *was* an asshole!

FRAN. And you're a *bitch*!

ELLEN. WHAT?

FRAN. A beach-bond *bish*! A beech-bonn—A bleach-blond blish! *(Stamps floor in frustration.)* A beesh—a *BEESH*!

ELLEN. *(Calmer now.)* Are you trying to say "Bleach-blonde bitch"?

FRAN. BITCH! BEACH-BOND BITCH! A BEACH! A BEESH BOSH BISH!

Scene 5
The Line That's Picked Up 1000 Babes, Part II

BENNY. In every stupid romantic comedy ever made, the guy falls in love with some girl who, by the movie's end, will see him for what he *really* is and therefore fall in love with him. *(Pause.)* This is bullshit.

ALAN. Okay.

BENNY. Hollywood just tells people what they want to hear. "All you have to do is be *yourself* ..."

No. Being yourself is a wonderful thing. *Knowing* yourself. But it's never going to get you the girl.

ALAN. Mmm.

BENNY. You know?

ALAN. Yeah. Especially if what you are is an asshole.

BENNY. Exactly! That is what I mean.

ALAN. So what happened?

BENNY. Over there? The girl?

ALAN. Well, yeah.

BENNY. Nothing.

ALAN. Well, *something* must have happened.

BENNY. What happened is that nothing happened. Didn't work out. Mistakes were made. You know? These things happen. You wash it off.

ALAN. Mistakes like what?

BENNY. Mistakes. First thing, and this was nothing I could have known in advance, was her name.

ALAN. What would that have to do with it?

BENNY. Well, her name was Ellen.

ALAN. So?

BENNY. I'm *telling* you. Her name was Ellen and that's a nice name, and she *was* a babe by the standards of the book ... but things could have been more to my advantage.

ALAN. If her name was different.

BENNY. Names are the key to many things. Especially for girls.

ALAN. You would have stood a much better chance if her name was Laura.

BENNY. *Laura*, hard to call. That's a toughie. But it's better than *Ellen*. Laura at least ends in a *vowel*.

ALAN. A vowel. That's important.

BENNY. You see? You should notice these things. Girls whose names end in vowels are a godsend. Especially "I."

ALAN. Like ...

BENNY. Kerri. Brandi. *Lori*. If her name is Laura but she calls herself "Lori," you're in.

ALAN. Debbi.

BENNY. Right! If her name is Debbi but she calls herself "Debra," forget it, no go. Especially is she goes beyond the world of "Debra" and starts calling herself "Deborah." Don't even *talk to* "Deborah."

ALAN. But Debbi ...

BENNY. I would kill at this point for a Debbi. The line would have absolutely worked on a D-E-B-B-I.

ALAN. Benny. The line didn't work. Okay? You're here, not there.

BENNY. Okay. Okay. I'll tell you. I failed with Ellen. See? I'm not ashamed. I SCREWED UP ELLEN. But listen. YOU do better. Fucking high-and-mighty KNOW-IT-ALL.

ALAN. Hey, I'm not in competition with you. What if I don't *want* to pick anybody up? What if?

BENNY. Well, I have no intentions of leaving with *you* tonight.

ALAN. Good luck.

BENNY. You really don't think the line works, do you?

ALAN. I don't even know what the line *is*, but no, I don't think it works. Lines aren't what get girls.

BENNY. Yes they do. The *right* line. And even the *best* line isn't going to always work. Just every so often.

ALAN. Every so often. I bet I can go up to a girl and say, "Let's go home and fuck," and it'd work "every so often."

BENNY. Yeah, but what would you be stuck with? Just some friggin' one-nighter.

ALAN. Oh. Yours is a line for a lasting relationship.

BENNY. All I'm saying is that my line works.

ALAN. I promised myself I wouldn't ask. *But.* What *is* this stu— ... Whoa.

BENNY. What? *What?*

ALAN. What about her over there?

BENNY. Who?

ALAN. That girl with the really long hair.

BENNY. Wh—*her?* Get out of here. That's no babe.

ALAN. Thank God.

BENNY. No way. You'd never have a chance.

ALAN. Why not?

BENNY. "Let's go home and fuck?" Are you serious? On a girl like her?

ALAN. What are you, an idiot? That was an example! It was an argument against the use of moronic pick-up lines. I have never said that. I never plan to. Okay? Got it?

BENNY. Oh.

ALAN. You really thought I'd *use* that line? That's so ridiculous. Excuse me, I'm going to go talk to that pretty girl now.

BENNY. You'll never make it.

ALAN. Is that what the book says or is that your opinion?

BENNY. Both.

ALAN. Why?

BENNY. Book says.

ALAN. Yeah, what does it say?

BENNY. Let me show you the difference between Ellen and your future rejection over there. That girl there, she's dressed to be attractive. Yes?

ALAN. Okay ...

BENNY. Nothing more, nothing less.

ALAN. Okay.

BENNY. *Ellen* was dressed to *attract*. She had a purpose. That girl has no right being here.

ALAN. This bar should be restricted to girls who wear too much make-up, is that what you're saying?

BENNY. Something to that effect.

ALAN. I can't believe I'm listening to this as if you're sane.

BENNY. Hey, who said this was easy? Book talks about how confusing it is, trying to figure out who's a babe and who isn't. Book says to just cut through the confusion and *experiment*.

ALAN. Experiment.

BENNY. Right.

ALAN. So, fine. I'm going to go experiment with her.

BENNY. Oookay. But it'll never happen.

ALAN. Fine.

BENNY. I'm telling you. There's a whole chapter on rejection in here.

ALAN. I imagine you read it a lot.

BENNY. Fine. I'm just telling you. Don't get your hopes up.

ALAN. Listen, you don't want to experiment, that's fine, but stop putting me down.

BENNY. I just got this book, I haven't had time to experiment yet.

ALAN. What if you gave your line to the girl at the jukebox and she fell swooningly in your arms, and the two of you had a mad, passionate night of romance and the two of you fell in love, what then? You never would have gotten to experiment.

BENNY. She's not supposed to fall swooningly anywhere.

ALAN. But what if she *di*—

BENNY. The book says that if she reacts that strongly to the line, then maybe you shouldn't have given her the line in the first place, and to get out of the situation as fast as possible. If she fell swooningly in my arms, I'd have to drop her.

ALAN. You have to be kidding.

BENNY. No. The book says—

ALAN. That book is saying that if someone actually likes you *back,* you're supposed to *reject* them?

BENNY. The information in this book—

ALAN. That book is a piece of *shit,* that's what I think.

BENNY. *The information in this book—*

ALAN. It's time-tested, I know, I know. So it's *time-tested* shit. It's still shit.

BENNY. So then don't go by it, see what I care! Go talk to her!

ALAN. I will, thank you.

BENNY. Good. Good luck. You're going to need it.

Scene 6
Seeing Teal

(ELLEN, FRAN, and CHARLIE are sitting silently, looking in three different directions. Long pause.)

CHARLIE. Bars like these are the social capitals of the world, you know. Friendliest places on earth.

FRAN. You must be judging by the company. Sorry ...

(Another long pause.)

CHARLIE. I'm really glad you invited me back over here. To think that I could be drinking by myself.

ELLEN. *(Suddenly.)* Fran, you know that dress, that teal skirt I lent you?

CHARLIE. "Teal?" That is one thing that separates guys from girls. Girls have this ... this extensive "color-vocabulary" thing. From reading too many Maybelline catalogs. What the heck is "teal?"

FRAN and ELLEN. Green!

CHARLIE. THEN SAY GREEN! Who made up this "teal" thing?

ELLEN. They're two entirely different colors. One has nothing to do with the other.

CHARLIE. No. My mom bought me Crayola crayons when I was a lid, the big 64-pack with the sharpener in the side and I never recall seeing "teal" in there.

ELLEN. *(Showing him something.)* This is teal.

CHARLIE. That is green.

ELLEN. Green is darker.

CHARLIE. Green is many different tints and shades of that color that resembles grass. If it's a notch up or down, it's still green.

FRAN. Ellen.

ELLEN. What?

FRAN. What about the skirt?

ELLEN. What fucking skirt?

FRAN. The teal skirt?

ELLEN. Oh yeah. I want it back.

FRAN. Fine. Fine.

(Pause.)

ELLEN. So. What else shall we talk about?

CHARLIE. Nothing colorful.

ELLEN. *I* know. Fran. Why don't you tell us what your new year's resolutions are.

FRAN. Huh—me? What are you talking about, this is April.

ELLEN. I mean not new *year*. New *age*. *(To Charlie.)* Her birthday.

CHARLIE. Happy birthday.

FRAN. *(Absently.)* Yeah.

ELLEN. So what are they?

FRAN. I've never in my life made new-age resolutions.

ELLEN. Well, you should. You could use some changing.

FRAN. Ahh, err, Charlie, how about buying me a drink?

CHARLIE. Or how about, "Charlie, go away for a while."

FRAN. Charlie, go away for a while.

CHARLIE. By God, I have this urge to, uh, go away for a while. *(HE leaves.)*

FRAN. Just what in God's name do you think you're doing?

ELLEN. What's your problem?

FRAN. Listen, if you want to hate Charlie, that's fine. If you want to hate *me*, that's fine, too. If you want to try to pick Charlie up, okay! If you want to drive him away, great! But I *do* wish you'd make up your mind about it!

ELLEN. Why should I drive him away when you want to fuck his brains out?

FRAN. ELLEN!

ELLEN. Oh don't Ellen me. Miss Little Girl. Doesn't come to know *bars,* doesn't want people to think she's a normal human being. Face the facts, kid, you're trying to pick him up! Say it!

FRAN. I am *not*—

ELLEN. Bullshit.

FRAN. Listen, I'm sorry I called you a bitch—

ELLEN. Oh, this has nothing to do with that. I *am* a bitch. And if you tell anybody I said that, I'll kill you, hear me? But I suppose you're kind of right, because what I'm about to do is a bitchy thing. I thought maybe I shouldn't, but I'm gonna.

FRAN. Wh— what are you going to do?

ELLEN. I'm leaving. Let's go home.

FRAN. What??

ELLEN. Yup, I guess it's about that time, huh? Ready to head on out, Fran?

FRAN. Boy, you are too much.

ELLEN. I'm also the driver of the car that you came in. So if *I* leave, *you* leave. ... unless you get someone *else* to drive you home. Or unless you go to someone *else's* home ...

FRAN. Ellen, please don't. I ... I don't know what I'm doing here. I—I just, *Ellen,* this isn't fair! Stay with me just to see what happens?

ELLEN. Oh, and if Charlie isn't as gung-ho about you as you'd like, *then* I get to take you home? Nice.

FRAN. But you *want* me to meet people, you always said.

ELLEN. Yeah. And now I want something else. I want you to admit you're trying to pick up Johnny Walker here.

FRAN. I'm *not,* I'm j—

ELLEN. Then why so upset to leave? Come on, let's go.

FRAN. *(Long pause.)* ... go ...

ELLEN. What was that?

FRAN. Go .... I'll get a ride.

ELLEN. You will, huh? Okay. I'd stand here and give you a chance to change your mind, except if I did that, you'd *change* your mind. Wouldn't you? *(FRAN looks at her.)* Stop, don't you open your mouth, you already answered. You're *here* now. And, I'll tell you. I think he likes you. You drive me crazy, you don't want to come here and then the guys wind up coming at *you*. Funny. Funny. So good luck. *(Shakes her head.)* Man. Shit. What's a nice girl like you doing in a place like this?

(ELLEN leaves. FRAN sits there by herself few moments. SHE takes a deep breath as the LIGHTS fade.)

Scene 7
A Challenge
(Ballad of a Nice Guy)

DIANE. I came here to meet a friend of mine who never showed. So here I am, by myself, in a bar, and what do you think happens?

ALAN. Everybody comes after you.

DIANE. Bingo. And now you.

ALAN. Come on. I don't use lines. Have I used a line?

DIANE. "I don't use lines" is the biggest line going.

ALAN. Okay, okay, I'm sorry, I'll go away.

DIANE. No no, no. Listen. I'll tell you what. You want me to believe that you're not like all the other guys here.

ALAN. Well ... yeah.

DIANE. And that's why I should go home with you.

ALAN. HUH? I never said—

DIANE. You never said, you never said, but you're shooting for the same things as everybody else, right?

ALAN. As everybody else. Including you: once you realized your friend wasn't showing up, why didn't you just go home? No, you're looking, too.

DIANE. Touché. But I'm looking for the right guy. Are you looking for the right girl?

ALAN. ... Yes.

DIANE. And I'm her.

ALAN. I don't know. How do I know? I don't know if you're the right girl, you don't know if I'm the right guy. Boy, you don't pull your punches, do you?

DIANE. *You* think you're the right guy.

ALAN. What's your—? I think I'm the right guy for *someone,* yeah.

DIANE. Okay. Prove it.

ALAN. Prove what?

DIANE. That you're the right guy for me.

ALAN. I don't know if I am.

DIANE. So we'll find out.

ALAN. How?

DIANE. How. Let's see ... Okay, tell you what. You talk for three minutes. Say whatever you want. Sell yourself. If I like what you have to say, I'll go home with you, if not, then, forget it.

ALAN. You'll ... now, wait just a minute.

DIANE. What?

ALAN. You'll go home with me?

DIANE. If I like what you have to say.

ALAN. If you like what I have to say, then I must be the right guy.

DIANE. Right. Ready to start?

ALAN. Is this how you always do things?

DIANE. Start when I say go ... Go.

ALAN. WHAT? Wait! I'm not... hey! I... uh... I—OKAY! My name is Alan—

DIANE. I know that already.

ALAN. Would you *SHUSH*?

DIANE. Sorry. Go.

ALAN. My name is Alan and ... *(ALAN goes utterly blank.)*

DIANE. *(After a pause.)* Just tell me what you're like—

ALAN. *(His frustration and anger builds gradually as HE delivers this.)* I'm a nice guy. I'm a goddamn nice guy. I say that not because *I* think it's true but because that's what everybody says. If you ask any girl who's known me for more than a week, that's how they'll describe me. "Alan? He's a nice guy." They say that because, you know, hell, *you* know nice guys, right? Don't try to *hurt* people, try to be a *gentleman.* Treat people right, especially girls. Because that's what we learned girls are attracted to, they want to be treated right. Right? You get a bunch of girls together and get them talking about guys, and they'll dream you up the perfect gentleman. But when it comes to real life, oh man!, that's very different. Because you get those girls together and get them talking about *real* men, not figments of their imagination but *real people,* and what do you get? *(Mimicking.)* "Ohhh, men are scum! Men are slime! Men are *shits!"* *(You* notice how all those words begin with "S"? I think there's something to that.) So men are all these "S" words, all these and more, but who do the girls date? Who comes on to them at the bars and who do they go home with? The *slime!* The *shits*! And then after they get hurt, and they always do, they call me up to confide in me, because long ago we decided that we were "just going to be friends." (I swear, you girls need to get a whole new vocabulary; you girls have started so many goddamn clichés it's not even funny.) So these girls call me up and they say "Alan, all guys are *sliiiime!*" and then they realize that they're *talking* to a guy, and they say, "Oh, except you, Alan, you're a Nice Guy. When you find a girlfriend, she's going to be such a lucky girl. But it can't be me because, well, I'm attracted to guys that are going to shit all over me." So great. So now I've got all the friends I need, so why should I be a nice guy anymore? Huh? I think I'll be a shit now. Yeah! I think I'll learn some stupid pick-up lines and use them on girls who are dressed to get laid. I think I'll be proud of how loud I can belch. I think I'll use women like they're Black and Decker screwdrivers! Sure! That's what girls *really* want to hear! So great! Life begins now, okay? OKAY? Come on, *babe,* let's go home and *FUCK*!

(Pause. ALAN is out of breath. Then:)

DIANE. Very commanding.
ALAN. Thanks.

(Pause.)

DIANE. Well. Goodbye.
ALAN. HUH?
DIANE. You lost. Goodbye.
ALAN. What? I—that's *it*? It's over?
DIANE. Yes.

ALAN. Does this mean you're not going home with me—

DIANE. You know what's amazing? I didn't think you were really going to go through all that.

ALAN. You told me to.

DIANE. You do everything people tell you to?

ALAN. Oh *man,* you are too much! What did you want me to do?

DIANE. I wanted you to do exactly what you did. I just didn't think you were going to. I was surprised.

ALAN. So that's *good!*

DIANE. No.

ALAN. No?

DIANE. No. I thought that if I let you simply tell me about yourself, I'd get some sincerity or something. I don't know what I was thinking.

ALAN. I was being goddamn sincere.

DIANE. About being a nice guy.

ALAN. YES!

DIANE. I'm sure you are.

ALAN. Then what in heaven's name is the problem?

DIANE. Throughout that whole thing, you were only telling me you were a nice guy so you could pick me up. You were using your disadvantages to your best advantage. And because your whole speech was nothing but some devious way to get me to like you, it wasn't truly sincere. And because it wasn't sincere, you really aren't a very nice guy at all. You want some girl to feel sorry for you because all the babes go for the guys with slick moves and mousse in their hair. Let me tell you—your whole nice guy thing is just one great big slick move. All you need now is the mousse.

ALAN. I don't believe this. What do you want to hear? What could I possibly have said to you that in your obviously hysterical state of paranoia, wouldn't have sounded like a line?

DIANE. There's no such thing.

(Pause.)

ALAN. How long ago did you just get dumped? Yesterday, day before that?

DIANE. Oh, fuck you.

ALAN. And instead of fucking killing them with a gun, what are you, you're trying to make every single guy feel like he's the shit of the earth.

DIANE. Nice meeting you. Bye.

ALAN. I BET YOU LEAVE HERE TONIGHT WITH SOMEONE! I bet after your anger is abated, some guy is going to compliment your breasts, and instead of spitting at him or dragging him down, you're going to think how cute he is! YOU DON'T HAVE THE CLARITY YOU THINK YOU DO! *(Pause.)* "Nice guy" is a cliche. "Nice guys finish last," blah blah blah. I've never heard of a "nice girl." Kind of makes you wonder, huh?

DIANE. What do we have to be nice about?

Scene 8
The New Age

FRAN. *So. So. (Pause.)* So, have you had a lot of one-night stands?

CHARLIE. *(Nearly chokes on his drink.)* That's a hell of a question to ask a guy in a bar. What are you trying to do, sober me up?

FRAN. I'm sorry. I don't know what to say. Forget it. ... but have you?

CHARLIE. Come *on.*

FRAN. Okay, okay, change the subject.

CHARLIE. To what?

FRAN. To ... your choice.

CHARLIE. *(After a pause.)* So ... Uh. Come here often?

FRAN. Oh come *on!*

CHARLIE. What?? What's the matter?

FRAN. That's not a topic, that's a goddamn *line.*

CHARLIE. It's not a line. I'm curious. *Do* you come here often?

FRAN. I asked first.

CHARLIE. *I* asked first.

FRAN. You did not ask first, I asked my question first.

CHARLIE. Well then I was the first person to ask my question second.

FRAN. Wh ... What?? I—

CHARLIE. Never mind. You answer my question and I'll answer yours, okay?

FRAN. Okay ... what was your question?

CHARLIE. If you came here a lot.

FRAN. Oh, no. I only came here one other time. That was enough. I went up to the bar to get a drink and this guy came over to me and he said — *(Mimics his superior, flirtatious tone.)* "HI!" in this way that implied what he was really saying was "Boy, are *you* lucky. Of all the girls here, I've decided to talk to *you!*" Lucky me. He said to me, "What's your name?" I said, "Fran." He said, "That's a beautiful name." Fran? Fran. The name my father gave me out of revenge when I wasn't born a boy. Fran is a lot of things but none of them beautiful. No. So, then he says, "Hey! You Italian?" I said, "No," and start to walk away, but he *grabs my arm* and says "Hey! You Irish?" "What is this? NO! Goodbye!" And he says, "So! What are you then?" "Nothing! I'm nothing!" I said. And he stopped, and he looked at me, and he said, "Oh. I guess you're right. You're nothing." And he smiled this *smile* at me that really made him king of the mountain. This *smile* that said that I was nothing because I wouldn't talk to him, this *GUY*. Men are bad enough, but there's nothing worse than *GUYS*. He called me nothing. This asshole with the top two buttons of his shirt open to show that he had *no* chest hair. This *guy* with his conceited, judgmental smile. Called me "nothing." Should that have bothered me? What he thought? Maybe not. But it did. So I left. If this is where this guy belongs, then it's not where I belong, so I left. And never came back 'til Ellen dragged me here tonight. And since then, I have this bias against guys I meet in bars. Maybe I shouldn't, but I do, there it is.

CHARLIE. Even me.

FRAN. *Especially* you.

CHARLIE. Oh. Great.

FRAN. *I* mean—I don't know what I'm doing, shit.

CHARLIE. We were doing better before.

FRAN. Yeah.

CHARLIE. Things got so *serious* all of a sudden.

FRAN. So what's the answer?

CHARLIE. Huh? What's the question?

FRAN. One-night st—

CHARLIE. *(Babbling.)* Oh, yeah, weh, I ... yeah, heh, nah.

FRAN. *(Pause.)* Well?

CHARLIE. Well what?

FRAN. What's the answer?

CHARLIE. I just said! No! No .... *well* ...

FRAN. What?

CHARLIE. No. No, that doesn't count. No one-night stands.

FRAN. What are you talking about?

CHARLIE. Nothing, don't worry about it.

FRAN. I want to know!

CHARLIE. Why? It's my past. I've got a past, you know, I wasn't placed here spontaneously for your benefit.

FRAN. I'm sorry, you're right.

CHARLIE. With girls, Christ!, they need to know all the gory details of past loves, a kind of *tally sheet*, I don't know.

FRAN. *(Annoyed.)* Okay.

CHARLIE. *(Pause. He may have gone a bit far.)* We all get hurt.

FRAN. Yes.

CHARLIE. Anyway, let me tell you. This "one-night stand" of mine, the woman in question, she was a Cosmopolitan girl. Or wanted to be. Nothing personal against your gender, Fran, but *Cosmopolitan* is the all-time worst magazine since the creation of the universe.

FRAN. Yeah, I bet you read *Playboy.*

CHARLIE. Okay. Okay. But *Playboy* occasionally does something with intelligence and style, whereas *Cosmo* is a never-ending flood of sleaze.

FRAN. How often do you *read Cosmopolitan*?

CHARLIE. "How to Pick Up a Man: When you first meet a man, playfully look down at his *crotch.* He will feel deliciously flattered." I just pick it up when I know there's going to be something in there worth laughing at.

FRAN. "How to Pick Up a Girl: Get yourself drunk, find some poor girl who's not used to getting attention around her much better-looking friend, make her laugh and forget she's in a bar, and then offer her a ride home."

(Pause.)

CHARLIE. You know, that sounds familiar.

FRAN. I don't know if I'm cut out for this.

CHARLIE. You need a ride home?

FRAN. You know I do.

CHARLIE. Yeah. You wanna go?

FRAN. With you? You're drunk—hey! You're *drunk*!

CHARLIE. I thought we already established that, yeah.

FRAN. How were you going to get home? You wouldn't be able to get your car out of the parking lot.

CHARLIE. I, eh, usually find someone to drive me home.

FRAN. Oh, that's good anyway.

CHARLIE. Yeah. Yeah.

(Pause.)

FRAN. You mean girls.

CHARLIE. Pardon?

FRAN. You usually find some girl to drive you home.

CHARLIE. Well, sometimes it's a—

FRAN. Oh *man*! Please let me be wrong about what I am thinking, okay! Just let me be wrong!

CHARLIE. What are you thinking?

FRAN. Nothing.

CHARLIE. Okay.

FRAN. *(Pause.)* Man. So what am I, your latest target? That guy over there uses a book, and *you* get drunk and have some girl be your driver, huh?

CHARLIE. Fran ...

FRAN. Am I right?

CHARLIE. No.

FRAN. Thank God.

CHARLIE. Except I'm lying.

FRAN. Great. Great.

CHARLIE. Fran ...

FRAN. Is this how you met *her*?

CHARLIE. Who—met who?

FRAN. The Cosmopolitan girl.

CHARLIE. Fran—

FRAN. *Did* you? You got drunk just enough so you couldn't drive and she drove you home.

CHARLIE. Yes. Yes, I'm sorry.

FRAN. And she hurt you.

CHARLIE. What?

FRAN. What did she do?

CHARLIE. That's none of your business. If I blew it with you, I am sorry, I am truly sorry, but—

FRAN. I want to know.

CHARLIE. Tough shit.

FRAN. How many other times?

CHARLIE. How many other times what?

FRAN. Have you done this?

CHARLIE. JESUS! Fran! I—

FRAN. Was she the first? The first time?

CHARLIE. Yes.

FRAN. But she hurt you!

CHARLIE. SHE LEFT! We had a really nice time and I really thought something was going to *happen*. My entire life seems to be waiting for something to fucking HAPPEN. But it didn't happen with her because she left the next fucking day. I felt sick that I felt anything towards her so soon. *(Pause.)* What, you thought only girls get used? Surprise.

FRAN. How long ago?

CHARLIE. Two months? Or so.

FRAN. If you got hurt this way, why are you back?

CHARLIE. Will you *let up*?

FRAN. It doesn't make sense.

CHARLIE. It doesn't make sense? It doesn't make sense? *I'll* tell you what doesn't make sense. What doesn't make sense is you staying here after telling me how much you hate this place, even after your friend leaves. THAT doesn't make sense.

(Pause.)

FRAN. So neither of us are making much sense.

CHARLIE. That's what happens in these places. You come in and see somebody and your hopes rise and your IQ drops thirty points. When you need somebody, you start walking into walls.

FRAN. I'm sorry I asked you so many questions.

CHARLIE. Yeah ... well, now you know my life story.

FRAN. I'm glad you told me, though.

CHARLIE. Good.

FRAN. I still don't know what to do. I can't seem to *think* ...

CHARLIE. Look, I'm sorry I did this stupid getting-drunk stunt. But if I had said, "Gee, you look like someone special and I'd like to get to know you better," you'd have just melted into my arms, right? *(Pause.)* I'm sorry if I insulted you, but there's no shame in being liked by somebody. Even here, even in this hole. And I think you like me, too. Or did. I don't know. This is up to you. You can either throw your drink in my face and storm out of here and get a *cab,* or you can be complimented that I like you, drive me home, and take things from there. Nothing will happen you don't want to have happen. I promise. But this is up to you.

(FRAN pauses, deep in thought. Then SHE takes her drink and throws it in Charlie's face.)

CHARLIE. So that's it then.

FRAN. No. I've just always wanted to do that. Give me your keys, let's get the hell out of this bar.

CHARLIE. You got it.

(THEY leave together.)

Scene 9
The Line That's Picked Up 1000 Babes
Part III

BENNY. Welcome back.

ALAN. Oh shut up.

BENNY. I told you.

ALAN. But *maybe* you weren't right.

BENNY. I knew I was.

ALAN. Bully for you.

BENNY. So what happened?

ALAN. We talked for a little bit.

BENNY. About?

ALAN. About why people come to bars like this.

BENNY. And what was the verdict?

ALAN. Neither of us knew.

BENNY. So then what'd you say?

ALAN. I don't know—what, you want to know the whole conversation?

BENNY. I want to know what line you used.

ALAN. I didn't use any damn line. We just *talked*.

BENNY. Uh-huh.

ALAN. Look, *you're* the one with the step-by-step guide, not me. She and I just *talked*.

BENNY. Ohh. So what'd you *say*? What was the first thing you said to her?

ALAN. "Hello."

BENNY. Har har. I mean, what'd you say to get her into a conversation? The very first thing?

ALAN. ... I told her I don't normally just walk over and start talking to strangers, but that I was giving it a shot because she was so ...

BENNY. So ... so good-looking.

ALAN. Well, yeah.

BENNY. So "pretty"?

ALAN. Yeah, yeah, what's your problem?

BENNY. That's so *sweet*!

ALAN. Look, asshole—

BENNY. "You're so pretty," that's what you said?

ALAN. Yeah. I was *honest,* so goddamn what? What would you have said to her?

BENNY. I told you, I wouldn't have ever talked to her.

ALAN. I mean, if you *did.*

BENNY. I wouldn't have.

ALAN. Jeeez—what about the girl by the jukebox, what'd you say to her?

BENNY. Exactly what the book says to. The line that's picked up 1000 babes.

ALAN. And what is that?

BENNY. "You're so pretty, I just had to talk to you."

(Silence. Dead dead silence. Then:)

ALAN. *No* way.

BENNY. You're allowed to substitute "cute" for "pretty," though. Which do you prefer?

ALAN. Let me see that.

BENNY. I'll show you, no problem.

ALAN. No, never mind, I believe you. I just used that moronic line?

BENNY. Naw. For you, it was just being *honest.* Right?

ALAN. Well, she was.

BENNY. You were being honest to your advantage.

ALAN. That's really what this book says to say?

BENNY. Chapter 2.

ALAN. Holy shit.

BENNY. You just didn't use it on the right girl.

ALAN. It wasn't a *line.*

BENNY. Ah, but it was. The girls here are all expecting one, so anything you say is a line. Might as well make it a good one.

ALAN. Jesus. I hate the bar scene. There's got to be an easier way.

BENNY. You want to borrow my book tonight?

ALAN. No! Yes. Jesus. Why don't people just *talk* to each other anymore?

BENNY. I really don't—wow, look at *her*!

ALAN. WHERE?

End of Play

The Midnight Moonlight Wedding Chapel

CHARACTERS

PETER

MISTY

MARIE

WALTER

MARVIN

JULIANA

TIME & PLACE

Late one Tuesday night.
A wedding chapel in Las Vegal, one of the many
such chapels along The Strip.

Scene 1

(PETER and MISTY enter, arms around each other, giggling)

PETER. Hello??

MISTY. We're getting married!

PETER. Hello!!

MISTY. Someone marry us!

PETER. Someone marry us before we collapse here! Hey!

MISTY. Oh. Oh. How did I get like this?

PETER. Those ... what were they?

MISTY. "Ambulance—

PETER. "Ambulance Chasers." Whoever names these drinks knows their stuff, I'll tell you.

MISTY. Hello??

PETER. *(Calling out.)* Hey! Where is someone! We can just go to another chapel, you know!

MISTY. No, no! I like this chapel!

PETER. It's the first one we saw. There are like a million others.

MISTY. "Midlight moon ... moonlight midnight ..." I like the name.

PETER. You like the name, you can't say it.

MISTY. I'll say it tomorrow.

PETER. You won't even remember it tomorrow.

MISTY. I'll still say it. "Midnight Moonlight Wedding Chapel." There, I said it now, I don't have to say it tomorrow.

PETER. Okay.

MISTY. I will, anyway, though.

PETER. Hello??

MISTY. I like the name.

PETER. Where the hell is the guy? He left his door open, he's—

MISTY. Maybe he's been *killed*!

PETER. If he has, we're not getting married here.

MISTY. HELLO, ARE YOU DEAD!!??

PETER. Look, look.

MISTY. What?

PETER. "Back in Five Minutes." He's not here.

MISTY. Where is he?

PETER. I don't know. He left. Maybe he makes house calls.

MISTY. A priest who makes house calls?

PETER. I don't think this guy's a real priest.

MISTY. Of course he is. Only priests marry people.

PETER. And rabbis, and, uh, shaman.

MISTY. And captains of ships.

PETER. I don't know. Maybe he went to marry random people on the street. Everyone's drunk, they won't know until morning.

MISTY. We should get married on a ship! Have the captain marry us!

PETER. We're in Nevada. We're landlocked.

MISTY. So let's go to ... let's go to MICHIGAN!

PETER. He left his door open.

MISTY. And get married on Lake *Erie!*

PETER. He left his door open, isn't he concerned about getting robbed?

MISTY. Who would rob a priest?

PETER. How about anyone who just lost his last dollar at craps?

MISTY. Don't be so serious now...!

PETER. I'm not being serious, you just asked—

MISTY. You're being boring.

PETER. I am *not*—

MISTY. You're the most boring drunk person I've ever met.

PETER. Boring drunk person?! I'm marrying you, aren't I?

MISTY. Mmmmm. Maybe you won't be boring on the honeymoon.

PETER. I'm never boring on honeymoons.

MISTY. We'll see.

PETER. We can see right now.

MISTY. No! I'm saving myself for my husband! *(This cracks her up.)*

PETER. I will be in fifteen minutes! *(HE is chasing her around.)*

MISTY. So you have to wait!

PETER. Let's skip the wedding. Let's live in sin.

MISTY. Nooooooo nooooo nooooooo...

PETER. I'll still divorce you tomorrow if you want anyway.

MISTY. We can't get divorced if we're not *married* ...

PETER. We'll lie. We'll tell him we're married. The judge.

MISTY. Nooooooo.

PETER. Let's just go back to my hotel now and...

MISTY. We can't lie, that's plagiarism!

PETER. Perjury.

MISTY. Yeah.

(MARIE enters.)

MISTY. Hello.

PETER. Hello.

MARIE. *Hel*lo. Well. I'm sorry, I just ran across the street for a drink. Wasn't expecting much business tonight.

PETER. Why?

MARIE. Because I don't have any reservations. You need a reservation to get married here.

MISTY. What?

PETER. But—

MARIE. Did you want to get married?

MISTY. Well, of *course* we did, this is a wedding chapel!

PETER. We're ... deeply in love.

MARIE. I was really just about to close up, you
know ... *(SHE looks at them.)* You drunk?

PETER. No! *(Pause.)* A slight buzz, you
know...

MARIE. I don't marry drunk couples. Helping
impulsive people ruin their lives is not why my
husband went into this business. You know what
I'm saying?

PETER. I hear you, certainly. But you see ...

MARIE. Why bring more misery into a world
already up to its ass in it?

PETER. This would not be misery, this would
be, if you could just stay open a little while longer,
it'd be *great.*

MISTY. We've come all this way just to get
married in this chapel, because we heard so ... so
much about it ...

MARIE. Came all this way?

PETER. Yes! I'm from back east!

MARIE. Flew out here for a quickie marriage,
eh?

PETER. Yeah, you can say that ...

MARIE. Most people come out here for quickie
divorces.

MISTY. I mean, there's no one *here,* can't you
just ... I mean, you can't get married by
YOURSELF!!

MARIE. Huh?

PETER. Nothing. She's a lit—we're somewhat
... it's a giddy night and all.

MARIE. Well—

PETER. What does a wedding go for here, anyway?

MARIE. One hundred fifty dollars.

PETER. I'll pay you three hundred.

MARIE. I like you.

PETER. You're a peach yourself.

MARIE. Three hundred, huh? All right, three hundred dollars. That'll be for the whole schmeer, including the potato flakes.

PETER. Potato flakes?

MARIE. Potato flakes. I use potato flakes instead of rice. Better for the environment.

PETER. You're going to throw potato chips at us?

MARIE. Not *me*, the attendants.

PETER. Oh, but—

MARIE. And they're not *chips*, they're *flakes*. Like instant mashed potatoes, you know?

PETER. Well, we can skip the potato flakes, we don't have any attendants.

MARIE. No witnesses?

PETER. No.

MARIE. Ah, well, you gotta have witnesses. This can't be done without witnesses.

PETER. Why not?

MARIE. State law! We've only got two or three laws regarding marriage, so we try to follow them best we can.

PETER. Awww, but—

MARIE. 'Sides, what if she woke up tomorrow and decided she had made a mistake? I know, sounds crass, but—

PETER. Well, you see, what we're doing, see—

MARIE. I once had this big rock star, I won't tell you his name but you'd know him. He comes in here with this gorgeous woman, I mean this *gorgeous* girl.

PETER. Uh-huh—

MARIE. Now, they're both a little bit sloshed, like you, and a little bit impulsive, like you, but they're determined to get married and *I'm* not going to stop them, right?

PETER. I guess.

MARIE. He's got two buddies serving as witnesses. So we go through the whole thing and they're all throwing rice around—this is before potato flakes—and they leave. Next morning, the guy is back here, he wants to bribe me for me to say I never married him. Well, *I* can't do that, how would that look?

PETER. I guess not too good.

MARIE. No! 'Course not. Probably his two witnesses decided to forget the wedding had taken place, but I couldn't just do that. And the *girl* sure hadn't forgotten she had just tied the knot to a rich and famous rock star, that's for sure! Ha! I think they were married thirty-six hours, and she got alimony to keep her at the style of living to which she'd become accustomed. Guess she got accustomed *fast*!

PETER. I ... I guess, maybe ...

MARIE. And here you can bet all these kids are looking up to this guy with his big long hair and all his records, but who does he turn out to be?

(Pause.)

PETER. I give up, who?

MARIE. A big jerk. I bet he even told her he loved her. I bet. Your man love you, honey?

MISTY. I don't think so.

MARIE. I'm *sorry*?

PETER. Yes, yes, see, uhh ... we have an unusual thing here. That's why we really don't need a witness.

MARIE. Yeah, why's that? You're saying *up front* you don't love her?

PETER. Right! See? That's why there's no problem! We're just getting married and then tomorrow we're getting divorced! We know this ahead of time. So, uh, you see ...

MISTY. We're just getting married to see what it's like.

PETER. Yeah, something like that.

MISTY. I've never *been* married.

MARIE. I don't believe it *feels* much different.

PETER. Still, it's ... I mean ...

MARIE. You telling me you're keeping me here past closing time so I can marry you so you can go get divorced tomorrow??

PETER. Four hundred dollars. Okay?

MARIE. And you're thinking that just throwing money at me is going to make me wanna—

PETER. Five hundred dollars.

(Pause.)

MARIE. Well, what the fuck.

PETER. We've got the money, that's not a problem.

MARIE. Hit it big, huh?

PETER. I won three thousand dollars in a slot machine. Four sevens, right across.

MARIE. Well, congratulations.

PETER. Thank you.

MARIE. Can't say I'm happy about this. I just don't like it.

PETER. Well, well, take the money and run, that's all. I've never won anything in my life and I intend to have the night of my life.

MARIE. You still need witnesses, though.

PETER. So *you* witness.

MARIE. Now I can't witness, I'm the one running the thing. You need a witness who just stands around and *witnesses*.

MISTY. *Awww ...*

PETER. All right. I have a friend, Walter. I think he went to 7-11 to get a beer while we're being married.

MARIE. I'm not too fond of drunken witnesses.

PETER. Well, I'll try to get to him before he goes too far, but you'll have to accept whatever we come up with. I mean, really, let's not be picky.

MARIE. Just my own personal rules. I've bent enough of them already. I'll throw in one more for free.

PETER. How about bending the witnesses rule altogether?

MARIE. Nope. That one's staying right where it is.

PETER. You're taking the spontaneity out of an otherwise beautiful thing, you know? If he's not at the 7-11, what am I supposed to do?

MARIE. Get married tomorrow and divorced the day after that?

PETER. Couldn't you just give me a break—?

MARIE. Well, I happen to know that there are other chapels within a stone's throw of here will marry you without witnesses. Chapel right up the road will marry you to a duck-billed platypus if that's your taste. I was about to close up anyway, so it's no skin off my back.

MISTY. No no no!

PETER. Aww, look. Can't you just—I mean. *(To Misty.)* Come on, let's go somewhere else.

MISTY. No, I like this place, Peter!

PETER. Well she's not going to marry us unless I go searching the city for Walter, what do you want? Let's go across the street to the Kentucky Bluegrass Chapel or something.

MISTY. I don't want to get married in a place that would marry you to a marsupial!

PETER. Well, if they're the only ones who'll... What the hell is a marsupial?

MISTY. Like a platypus.

PETER. *What?*

MARIE. No, now, a platypus isn't a marsupial, it's a mammal just like you. Now if you said *"kangaroo—"*

PETER. Excuse me! Can we veer back to the subject at hand?

MISTY. I just want to get married here, please, Peter?? Following all the rules and everything. We can find a witness. Get Walter.

PETER. He's probably back at a slot machine somewhere. God knows where he is.

MISTY. Please...?

PETER. If I can't find him, what am I supposed to do, accost strangers? I'll tell you, why don't we just forget it, go back to my hotel room, hmmm? And continue with our victory celebration, huh?

MISTY. *(Disappointed.)* Ohhhh ....

PETER. It'll be fun. We can pretend we're married. We can pretend anything we want.

MISTY. I guess, but ...

PETER. I know, but if I can't find Walter, what am I supposed to do? C'mon, let's just go.

MISTY. I suppose.

PETER. Okay. *(To Marie.)* All right? You happy now? We're not getting married. So much for five hundred dollars.

MARIE. Well, least I can close up shop.

PETER. Fine, you do that.

MISTY. It's just that, I mean ... what about the perfect night?

PETER. So it won't be a perfect night, it'll be just be a *really good* night.

MISTY. Yeah, but ... we were going to have the best night of our entire lives. *(Pause.)* I mean, right? You said you haven't had fun since 1983. And, I mean, me either! I'm sorry, I'm just disappointed.

(Pause.)

PETER. That's not what I said. I've done fun things in the last decade.

MISTY. But, you said—

PETER. No, what I *said* was I haven't really let *loose.* I've had *fun,* though. God. I go to movies, I go to bars, I play basketball. Don't make it sound like I've been locked in my room all this time. I admit I haven't met a cocktail waitress and married her on the spot before. And *that* might have made this into a perfect night. Which is what I'm ENTITLED to after the last few years of, of ... All right, okay. Stay right here, the wedding's back on.

MISTY. You mean it??

MARIE. Now, wait, you just said—

PETER. Yeah yeah yeah, I'm sorry, but I made a promise here. All right? Six hundred dollars, and that's my final offer.

MARIE. Six hundred and fifty.

PETER. You're crazy! A wedding costs a hundred and fifty dollars!! *(Pause.)* Ohhhh, boy, you're lucky I'm in a good mood here ... I'm getting Walter. Don't close up.

MARIE. No sir. Don't take forever, though.

PETER. Yeah yeah, or the price'll go up. *(To Misty.)* Stay here. I'll be right back. *(PETER exits.)*

(Pause.)

MARIE. Quite a find there, honey.
MISTY. He's sweet.
MARIE. So, uhh ... what is your name?
MISTY. Misty.
MARIE. Misty, eh?
MISTY. Misty Sunday Merriwether. *(Pause. Conspiratorily.)* That's not my real name.
MARIE. Oh?
MISTY. I changed it because I wanted to be a dancer and I figured I'd need a, you know, a stage name.
MARIE. I see.
MISTY. Oh this is all so exciting! Getting married ...
MARIE. It's a very unusual thing, what you're doing.
MISTY. Oh, I know, I know! But you know ...
MARIE. What.
MISTY. I never do anything.
MARIE. What?
MISTY. I mean, I *eat* and stuff. Like Peter says he still has fun sometimes, but, I mean ... Like, I play slot machines—ten dollars out of every paycheck. No more. And I don't put my winnings back in again, either, I keep them. That's how the casinos make their money you

know, from people winning money and giving their money right back. So I do that and I waitress at the Tropicana. And guys try to pick me up, and sometimes I go out with other waitresses, but that's, like, what we go out and do is pretty much the same as *our jobs.* I mean, I thought Vegas was going to be really exciting when I first moved here, to be a dancer, but it really isn't, you know? So I really don't do much. Waitress. Audition. Do the slots. Slots are all I really like because it's all fate, just you and the machine, right? I can always feel which slot machine is going to pay off. It's like I always know which way to go. That's how I met Peter, I told him which machine to play, and he did and he won all that money, so we got drunk and then we decided to do this. This is the most fun I've had in a long time. Thank you for not closing! I mean that.

MARIE. You're quite welcome.

MISTY. How many people do you marry?

MARIE. In a day?

MISTY. Yeah.

MARIE. Oh, a lot. Sometimes as many as a hundred people.

MISTY. Do they let you know how they're doing?

MARIE. I'm sorry?

MISTY. Do they ... I don't know, drop a card ... "Hi, we're still married," things like that?

MARIE. No, I'm afraid not.

MISTY. Oh. Aren't you curious?

MARIE. I can't really say I've thought about it. I do fear that many of the marriages end in divorce. Some the next day. I do believe you're the first couple to *plan* it that way, though.

MISTY. I hope you don't mind.

MARIE. Mind? I guess not. This is your life. It's just been so long since I married two people I thought might last. Seems I'm always giving vows to some seventy-five-year-old man and his twenty-year-old bride. I think the longest-lasting marriage I've done was when I married this guy's dog to this other woman's cat.

MISTY. The people weren't married?

MARIE. The people didn't want to get married. They were living together. I married their pets. Don't ask. It took forever to get the cat to meow when it was supposed to say "I do."

(PETER enters, with WALTER.)

WALTER. ... I don't understand ...

PETER. I'll explain after, just shut up and *observe.*

MISTY. Hi again.

WALTER. Hi.

MARIE. All right.

PETER. I found him.

WALTER. I'm still confused.

PETER. I am going to marry Misty and you're going to watch me do it.

WALTER. Well, if you ask me—

PETER. No one's asking you anything.

WALTER. This is the stupidest idea I have ever heard in my entire life.

PETER. Fine.

WALTER. Can't you have a *normal* one-night stand? *(To Misty.)* No offense, but I guess you know you're a one-night stand. I mean, you're breaking up *tomorrow*.

PETER. Are you going to witness or not?

MARIE. I need you all to sign this ...

WALTER. You know what? No. I'm not witnessing.

PETER. What??

WALTER. I think it's a ridiculous mistake and I don't see why I should participate.

PETER. That's the point—you're not participating, you're *witnessing*

WALTER. I'm not even doing that.

PETER. Oh fer God's ...

WALTER. I mean, I mean ... marriage is a sacred *institution*.

PETER. *(To Misty.)* And you thought I was a boring drunk?

WALTER. It is. And what you're doing is only going to lead to dire consequences for yourself—

PETER. —dire consequences, who *talks* like this?—

WALTER. —*for yourself* and God knows who else. So, no. No. Nope.

MARIE. Well, I'm very sorry then, but in that case—

PETER. HOLD it. If my *ex*-friend doesn't want to be my witness then by goodness I'm going to go out and get one.

WALTER. Yeah? Where?

PETER. Let me think.

MARIE. You really don't have anyone around to serve as a witness?

PETER. I'm here on vacation from New York, everyone I know is back East. I have an Uncle Horace lives in Sacramento, California, I can fly him out here if you friggin' want.

MISTY. You'd *do* that??

PETER. NO I WOULDN'T DO THAT!

MARIE. What do you do back in New York?

PETER. I'm a medical editor. I edit medical texts.

WALTER. He takes out appendixes.

PETER. That joke is getting so old.

WALTER. C'mon, do the other half.

PETER. I also take out colons.

MARIE. Cute.

MISTY. I thought you guys had professional witnesses.

MARIE. Sometimes, yes. Daytimes. Weekends. By request, in advance. Tuesday night at midnight my witnesses are all home sleeping.

WALTER. *(To Peter.)* Why don't you just skip this, anyway. You know it's dumb.

PETER. No, now I *want* to do this. You still want to do this, Misty?

MISTY. Yeah!

PETER. All right then. This is *my night* goddammit, I'm the winner and I'm going to get married to this beautiful girl. For a while.

WALTER. Yes, well we see how great your last marriage went.

PETER. *(Annoyed.)* Hey!

WALTER. And who's the one said it wouldn't work? Why ... it was me! I'm telling you, Pete, you gotta listen to me or suffer the consequences.

PETER. You. Yeah, my role model. If a girl calls you twice in the same week you change the phone number. Now I *deserve* a night like this, dammit, and I'm going to find a witness if it kills me.

MARIE. We had this one guy hired a hooker to serve as a witness.

PETER. A hooker? That's a great idea! Hire a hooker!

MARIE. Of course, he was *marrying* a hooker...

PETER. Oh, great. Where are these hookers?

MARIE. I'm surprised you didn't trip over them as you came in.

PETER. Good! I am off to get a prostitute!

MISTY. Peter ...

PETER. What?

MISTY. ... I know you want to do this ...

PETER. What's the matter?

MISTY. ... but ...

PETER. WHAT? What?

MISTY. Can't we get someone other than a hooker?

PETER. What do you *want* from me here?

MISTY. It's just like ... I don't know ...

PETER. I mean, who else am I supposed to get?

MISTY. But a *prostitute* ... !

PETER. Look, let me go see, huh? If I don't have to get a hooker, I won't, but if there's no one else, let me do what I gotta *do* already, huh?

MISTY. I guess ...

PETER. All right. I'll be back in a bit. *(To Walter.)* You can go fuck yourself.

WALTER. I'm sorry, buddy, but my conscience just would not forgive me.

PETER. Fine. Next time you need a fiver to cover your lunch-room crap games, think about your conscience. Or when I told that girl you didn't want to talk to that you were in the hospital. Think about favors *then*.

WALTER. Sorry, man.

PETER. All right, I'll be right back.

WALTER. Hurry back.

PETER. What are you, staying here?

WALTER. Hell, yeah! I may not be helping, but I want to see what you come back with at one o'clock in the morning.

MARIE. Sir, I must insist it be soon. I was planning—

PETER. To close up, yes, okay, for six hundred and fifty dollars you can cut me some slack.

MISTY. Peter?

PETER. What?

MISTY. If it has to be a hooker...?

PETER. Yeah?

MISTY. Don't get one who looks like she dyed her hair.

(Pause.)

PETER. Right. Whatever you say. Be back in a few, guys. *(PETER exits.)*

(Pause.)

WALTER. So, what shall we do? Have a deck of cards? I can practice my blackjack.
MARIE. I don't have any cards.
WALTER. That's okay, I do. You in for a quick hand of poker?
MARIE. No, thank you. I'm going to take care of some things I should do. Tell me when he gets back.
MISTY. I'll play.
WALTER. Oh give me a break.
MISTY. No, I'll play, really.
WALTER. For money?
MISTY. You said practice.
WALTER. Fine, whatever. What do you want, five-card draw?
MISTY. How about blackjack?
WALTER. Whatever. Blackjack.
MISTY. Okay.
WALTER. *(Shuffles, deals.)* One down ... Jack up for the lady.
MISTY. Blackjack.

(Pause.)

WALTER. Anyone for solitaire? Why yes, thank you for asking. *(Deals solitaire for himself.)*

(Long pause.)

MISTY. Why don't you like me?

WALTER. I like you just fine.

MISTY. You seemed to before but now you don't.

WALTER. Hey, I don't care about you one way or another, all right?

MISTY. Then why'd you ask me out back at the casino?

WALTER. Oh please. I'm not allowed to ask out women unless I *care* for them? You think Peter cares about you?

(Pause.)

MISTY. Yes.

WALTER. Oh, well, please. I'm sure you're very nice but give me a break, you act like you flushed your brain down a toilet. How many guys have cared for you in the past six months? Did they all care for you? I mean, I can't tell if you're kidding me here or whether you really believe it. I don't mean to sound harsh, but I think the guys who pick you up when you're in an outfit like that, they care about one thing only.

MISTY. You tried to pick me up; you care about one thing only?

(Pause.)

WALTER. Hey. I'm here to have a good time, all right? I'm on vacation.

MISTY. And you probably think I'm in here getting married every other day, right? With guys on vacation.

WALTER. I don't know. It'd be your right, who could stop you?

MISTY. Well, I don't. I don't get married every night, I don't get laid every night—

WALTER. Oh, poor baby, that must be rough—

MISTY. I don't mind! *I* don't care whether I do or I don't. I'm not like a guy, I can actually *not have sex* for periods of time. I can't half the time because everyone here is, like—I mean, you think I'm *attracted to* guys like *you*? Come here with five hundred dollars, think you're a high roller, think because you're drunk and won a few bucks that means you can grab at me?

WALTER. I didn't grab at you.

MISTY. No, you just stared at me. You're even worse. At least the grabbers know they don't have a chance. You stood there staring at me like you were planning your move. You people creep me out.

(Pause.)

WALTER. And Peter's, what, a saint?

MISTY. No. I know I'll never see him again after this.

WALTER. Damn right.

MISTY. But I just want to feel like a normal person tonight. *(Pause.)* Never mind. Never mind. I just want to feel like a person. Because I didn't flush my brain down any toilet.

(Long pause. WALTER stares at her, and maybe he's about to say something more, but then MARVIN enters.)

MARVIN. Excuse me, are you open?

WALTER. What?

MARVIN. *(Imploringly.)* Would you marry me?

WALTER. *(Startled.)* Would I ... are you talking to me?

MARIE. *(Enters.)* Can I help you?

MARVIN. Are you open here?

MARIE. Not officially, no.

MARVIN. Are you the minister?

MARIE. Yes I am.

MARVIN. Ma'am, you'd be doing me the most incredible service if you would just simply—

MARIE. That's fine, okay, come in.

MARVIN. *(Calls out.)* JULIANA, I FOUND ONE.

MARIE. *(To Walter and Misty.)* I mean, at this point, what the hell.

MARVIN. You're doing us just the most incredible service, miss, uh ...

MARIE. Just call me Marie.

MARVIN. Marie.

(JULIANA comes in.)

MARVIN. *(To Juliana.)* See? I told you I'd find one.

JULIANA. Yes, you did.

MARVIN. *(To Marie.)* Okay. Go ahead. Start!

MARIE. Whoooa, hang on there. Nice to see a guy so gung-ho but we got to take care of a few things first.

MARVIN. Well, let's take care of them.

MARIE. Okay, well. First thing is, you guys got witnesses?

MARVIN. Yessir, you bet—a good five-hundred people saw me ask her hand in marriage.

MARIE. Well, that's very romantic, but it's not what I meant ...

MARVIN. You shoulda seen it, I was like a totally different person.

MARIE. Any of those five hundred happen to be *around* still?

JULIANA. He climbed up on to the craps table and bent down on one knee and asked my hand in marriage. Have you ever heard of such a thing?

MARVIN. Had to do it fast, too, because these bodyguards the size of race horses were trying to grab me off the table.

JULIANA. This Spanish croupier was trying to hit him with that stick-thing of his.

MARVIN. We've been seeing each other for eight years—

JULIANA. Eight years!

MARVIN. *Thirteen* years if you count how long we lived in the same town. But that's a different sort of seeing each other, you know?

JULIANA. No, those first five years, we just sort of *set our eyes* on each other.

MARVIN. I always knew she was there, though.

JULIANA. Yes. I knew we would date one day, and then we did!

MARVIN. But neither of us ever thought—

JULIANA. Marriage! I mean, *marriage!* Can you stand it? Eight years and now—

MARVIN. It took us this long to realize it.

JULIANA. All these years of seeing each other.

MARVIN. You know?

WALTER. Well, God, we sure do now.

MISTY. That's just the sweetest story!

MARIE. Well, I'll be happy to oblige you.

MARVIN. We really appreciate it.

MARIE. But I'm going to need a witness. State law.

MARVIN. Well, how about one of you? Would you mind?

WALTER. Oh ...well. *(To Misty.)* Peter would *kill* me.

MISTY. I could, though! That'd be great!

MARIE. Well, that's fine then, we'll sign the certificate after the service, that okay with everyone?

MARVIN. Okay!

JULIANA. Okay!

MARIE. All right, let me get my robe on and we'll get this started.

MARVIN. Well, we're going to do this.

JULIANA. Yes, we are.

MARVIN. You're not having any ... last minute thoughts, are you?

JULIANA. What?

MARVIN. I mean ...

JULIANA. I'm not if you're not.

MARVIN. Well, I'm not.

JULIANA. Well, then.

MARVIN. I'm not if *you're* not.

JULIANA. Well, *I'm* not.

MARVIN. Well, good, then.

JULIANA. Good.

MARVIN. Good.

JULIANA. Good.

MARVIN. I mean—

JULIANA. —what?

MARVIN. We're *ready*, right?

JULIANA. *I* think so.

MARVIN. I think so, too.

JULIANA. So we're ready.

MARVIN. (*To Marie.*) We're ready!

MARIE. Okay. Then why don't you stand there and you stand here ... fine. Now, what is your name?

MARVIN. Marvin Quigley.

MARIE. And yours?

JULIANA. Juliana-Elizabeth Holtsfield.

MARIE. Okay, Juliana. That's a very pretty name. Why don't you take this little bouquet of flowers then ...

JULIANA. Oh, thank you!

MARIE. And let us begin: We are gathered here on this evening to join Mar—

MISTY. *(Overlap.)* Morning.

MARIE.—vin Quig ... What?

MISTY. It's morning.

WALTER. Would you be quiet and let the lady do her work?

MISTY. Well, I don't want to get to the very end and not have it *count*!

MARIE. Don't worry, we're allowed a little room for error. But, anyway: We are gathered here this morning to join Marvin Quigley and Juliana-Elizabeth Holtsfield, two people who wish to express and bind their love together in front of these good people and the state of Nevada. Do you, Marvin, take this woman, to love and cherish, to honor and obey, in sickness and in health, good times and bad, til death do you part?

(PETER has entered at some point in Marie's speech.)

PETER. What the hell is going on??

MISTY. Peter!

PETER. Who are these people?

MARIE. Sir, I must ask your respect, there is a wedding taking place.

PETER. Yeah! Mine! What the hell?

MARVIN. Who's this guy?

PETER. Who am I?? Who are *you*?

WALTER. Pete, they're getting married.

PETER. What happened to our wedding??

MARIE. You two will be next.

MARVIN. Yeah, wait your turn!

PETER. Wait my *turn*? Hey, guy, I've *been* here for half an hour now.

MISTY. *Peter!*

WALTER. Did you get the prostitutes?

JULIANA. WHAT?

MARVIN. *Prostitutes?*

PETER. I couldn't get one over here, can you believe it? I always thought hookers didn't *like* sleeping with men, that they did it for money, only. So here I'm thinking I'm about to make some lucky hooker's *night*—they don't have to *do* anything, they can take it easy. But I go up to ten prostitutes and when I suggest they serve as witnesses at a marriage, they look at me like I'm going to tie them to the back of a moving freight train. I mean, was this such an outrageous proposition? I would think they hear a lot stranger over the course of the average night, right? *(Pause.)* Basically, when you get right down to it, I cannot remember a time when I could ever say I understood women. Period.

(Pause.)

MARVIN. *(To Marie)* Should I call the police?

MARIE. No, no. *(To Peter.)* Sir, these people really *do* want to get married, for good and forever, and I am honored to oblige them. I promise you, let me get through with this wedding, *maybe* five minutes, and I'll be right with you.

PETER. *(To Walter.)* Don't you tell me you're witnessing for these people?

MISTY. No, I am.

(PETER looks at her, surprised.)

WALTER. And, hey, if I *was* witnessing, at least I'd be watching two people who *love* each other. Not two random people who've lost their minds.

PETER. Lost our minds, huh? You don't even know the half of it. *(To Marvin.)* All right. What's your name?

MARVIN. My name?

PETER. Hell with it, I don't care what your name is. How much do you want?

MARVIN. How much do I want?

PETER. How much money do you want?

MARVIN. How much *money* do I want? To do what?

PETER. To stop repeating my questions.

MARVIN. What??

PETER. All right, scratch that. Look what I'm willing to offer you. I will give you ... two hundred and fifty dollars—

WALTER. WHAT?? Are you out of your—

PETER. TWO HUNDRED AND FIFTY DOLLARS to serve as my witness since my schmuck of a friend here is trying out for Popehood and can't besmirch his good name.

WALTER. Oh fuck you.

MARVIN. You're going to give me—

PETER. Two hundred and fifty dollars. For basically standing there.

MARVIN. Okay. Okay, maybe we can do this.

PETER. Plus, we go first.

MARVIN. Okay.

PETER. *Thank* you.

MISTY. Peter ...

PETER. Don't even start in with me.

MISTY. Are you sure you want to just give away all that money?

PETER. You know what? *(Hands money to Marvin.)* I just did. All right. Let's get this thing going finally.

MARIE. Well, okay. This has been some night. All right. If no one has any further objection...? Okay, then, if the two of you will step forward ... Your name is?

PETER. Peter Gatesman.

MARIE. We are gathered here this evening to join Peter Gatesman and Misty Sunday Merriwether, two people who wish to express and bind their love together in front of these good people and the state of Nevada. Do you, Peter, take this woman, to love and cherish, to honor and obey, in sickness and in health, good times and bad, 'til death—err. *(Pause.)* Well whatever, 'til death do you part?

PETER. I do.

WALTER. Can you believe this is legal?

(Various PEOPLE shush Walter.)

MARIE. And do you, Misty, take this man, to love and cherish, to honor and obey, in sickness and in health, good times and bad, 'til death do you part?

MISTY. I do!

MARIE. And does anyone present here have any reason to oppose this union? If so let him step forward now or forever hold his peace.

(WALTER strains not to speak.)

MARIE. Then by the power invested in me by the state of Nevada and the city of Las Vegas, I pronounce you man and wife. You may kiss the bride. Congratulations, please sign this certificate of marriage.

(PETER and MISTY do.)

MARIE. If you want this framed it's an extra fifty bucks.

PETER. That's quite okay.

MARIE. Have a nice day, then.

(MARIE, MARVIN, JULIANA, and WALTER throw potato flakes. Wedding MUSIC rises and the LIGHTS black out.)

End of Scene 1

Scene 2

(The next day, around noon.
PETER slams in to the chapel, followed by a more subdued WALTER.)

PETER. IS SHE HERE? I DON'T SEE HER. CHRIST!

WALTER. Peter, if you don't stop screaming I'm going to kill one of us. Probably me.

PETER. Where's the minister? Where is she?

MARIE. (*Enters from a back room.*) Ye—?

PETER. THERE you are. Was she here? Misty. The girl I married yesterday. Remember? Was she here? Was Misty here?

MARIE. Now hold on a sec—

PETER. GODDAMMIT SHE WASN'T HERE. Oh my God. Oh my God.

WALTER. Pete, you gotta get a grip on yourself.

PETER. Are you kidding? MY WIFE IS MISSING! She's gone! What am I supposed to do about that??

WALTER. We'll figure something out if we just stay—

PETER. *(A new thought.)* OH MY GOD!

WALTER. What???

PETER. I'm already married! I *have* a wife! I'M A BIGAMIST!

WALTER. What? No you're not, you're divorced.

PETER. Oh, yes. That's right. You're right. Thank you.

WALTER. You're going to have a stroke.

PETER. I can't even remember her last name.

WALTER. Wasn't it, like ... "Saturday"?

PETER. I don't know. A day or a month or something.

MARIE. No, that wasn't her real name, that was her stage name.

PETER. Oh God, she's right. I don't even know my wife's name.

WALTER. No, wait ... I remember ... it was ... Agh! Give me a minute.

PETER. Where did she go? God, God ...

WALTER. Her name was ...Juliana-Elizabeth Holtsfield!

PETER. What??

WALTER. No?

PETER. That doesn't sound right.

WALTER. I'm pretty sure it's a name.

PETER. I'd bet you anything it's a name, it's just not *her* name.

MARIE. When did you last see her?

WALTER. Yeah, trace back your steps.

PETER. She's not a set of car keys, dammit. I know where she was—in my bed!

WALTER. Are you sure?

PETER. What do you mean am I sure?

WALTER. Did you make it to the bed?

PETER. It's where I woke up. What are you getting at?

WALTER. I mean, you were really drunk last night. Did *she* get to your bed? You could have passed out, she could have taken your wallet and your keys and stolen your car. She could be halfway across the country now.

PETER. Walter. We drove here in my car. Which I operated with my keys. Here is my wallet.

WALTER. Yeah, but she COULD have.

PETER. All right. *(To Marie.)* Lady, can you just do me a favor, if she comes back here, can you have her call me? Here. *(HE writes something down.)* This is my number at the hotel.

MARIE. Sure thing, hon.

PETER. I appreciate it. This whole thing has gotten totally out of hand.

(MARVIN and JULIANA enter.)

WALTER. Hey, and here's happy-married couple number two! *(With a mock microphone, to Marvin:)* What's your secret to a long-lasting marriage?

MARVIN. *(To Marie.)* Can you tell us where to go to get a divorce?

PETER. Oh, it's the county courthouse; you just take the bus up about a mile and half.

WALTER. I'm going back to sleep.

MARIE. *(To Marvin.)* WHAT did you just say?

MARVIN. Is that on the right side or the left side?

PETER. I don't know. The right side, I think.

WALTER. Peter!!

PETER. What??

WALTER. Don't help, okay? Just concentrate on your own problems.

PETER. They asked a question, I was helping out.

WALTER. Just—just sit down, okay?

MARIE. Why the change of heart there, folks?

JULIANA. I changed my mind. I changed my mind.

MARVIN. No. No, it was me. We were up all night talking, and, and ...

MARIE. Your wedding night, that's not what you're supposed to be doing.

MARVIN. What? Oh. Yes. But no, we were talking, and we came to the conclusion that maybe we rushed things a bit.

WALTER. WHAT??? You guys have been seeing each other since the goddamn turn of the century and you think that you're ... I can't even think of how—I mean ... you *rushed* this?

MARVIN. I know what you're thinking.

WALTER. You couldn't possibly know what I'm thinking. My friend here—say hi, Peter—my friend here married someone yesterday, someone he met two hours before the ceremony. Okay? THAT is rushing things. Do you see? Do you see the difference? THAT'S what I'm thinking.

MARVIN. You really did that?

PETER. Yes.

MARVIN. Why?

PETER. We were just getting divorced the next day. It was all a joke.

MARVIN. That's terrible!

WALTER. *Thank* you.

PETER. Yeah, well, what do you want.

MARVIN. Then what are you doing here?

PETER. I can't find her. She's totally missing.

MARVIN. She's missing?

PETER. (I thought maybe she came back here for some reason ...)

MARVIN. I think God is teaching you a lesson.

PETER. Oh, good. Well why doesn't he teach me *math* or something I can *use*. Fat lot of good teaching me "Don't marry someone you're going to divorce the next day." He thinks I do this a *lot*? Walter, let's go, she's not here.

WALTER. Wait wait wait, wait a second.

PETER. Walter! Can we stick with our own situations?

WALTER. Give me a minute, okay? Give me five minutes.

MARIE. If you folks thought you were rushing things, why did you come all the way out here then? I mean, what happened after you left here that didn't happen on the plane ride in, or in the casino, or ...

WALTER. ... the previous thirteen years.

MARIE. Yeah.

MARVIN. My darn police scanner.

(Pause.)

MARIE. Is that an answer?

JULIANA. He's loved listening to his police scanner for as long as I remember.

MARVIN. I bought it when I was twelve, sat and listened to it—

JULIANA. All day! This is only when we were friends, now. But then when we started becoming romantically involved, he listened to it less—

MARVIN. —there were other things more important—

JULIANA. But still a lot! More than the average person, I think, listens to a police scanner or is *supposed* to listen to a police scanner.

MARVIN. But she didn't mind.

JULIANA. No, I did not.

MARVIN. Anymore than I minded when she made her little wire figurines.

JULIANA. I make little wire figurines.

MARVIN. They look like these little pipe cleaners from hell.

JULIANA. They get on his nerves.

MARVIN. They're just *everywhere* in her house.

JULIANA. I make a lot of them. It's a hobby.

MARVIN. She makes them special for the person who wants 'em. Freelance.

JULIANA. I ask them what they do, or what they like to do. If they golf, I make them a little wire golfer. You see?

MARVIN. They all look exactly the same. Golfers, truck drivers, businessmen. They all look—

JULIANA. Oh they do not.

MARVIN. There was one that looked different: She had one guy say he was a sculptor, so she wadded up this great hunk of wire and handed it to him. "What's that?" he asked. "It's a hunk of marble made out of wire," she said.

JULIANA. He bought it though.

MARVIN. She makes ten dollars a month.

JULIANA. How much do you make listening to your police scanner? WHICH, by the way, he takes out first thing when we get back to our honeymoon suite.

MARVIN. I know, and that was wrong.

JULIANA. It's okay. It is! But I knew then that all this time we were fooling each other. A thirteen year practical joke.

MARVIN. And when she explained it to me, I knew it, too.

JULIANA. Right when he pulled out the scanner I realized that I had jumped at Marvin way back when because he was the first to ask me out on a date. And things just kept railroading along, date after date, until suddenly here we are married and asking for a divorce. Time does fly, doesn't it?

MARVIN. We never gave anyone else even a chance.

JULIANA. I realized it last night. I don't want a man in my life. I want THE man, I want the RIGHT man. And maybe it's Marvin and maybe it's not. How do I know? I don't.

MARVIN. And I don't know any other woman, not one.

JULIANA. We have to see.

MARVIN. So, that's it then.

JULIANA. *(To Marie.)* It's nothing personal against you.

MARIE. No. No offense taken. I'm just a little ... I don't know. You seemed so happy. Umm. Do you have your marriage certificate?

JULIANA. Yes, see. We need this to get divorced?

MARIE. I believe so.

(PETER grabs the certificate out of Juliana's hands.)

PETER. Oh my God!!

JULIANA. Hey!

MARIE. What are you—??

PETER. Look! Misty signed her real name here!!

WALTER. What? Oh my God.

PETER. Gladys Kravitz.

WALTER. Jesus. No wonder she changed it.

PETER. I know her name now! I can go see if she's in the phone book! *(To Marie.)* Can I use your phone?

MARIE. In the back, right there.

PETER. Thanks. *(HE starts to leave.)*

MARVIN. Can we have the certificate back please?

PETER. Oh! Right. Here.

WALTER. *(Grabs the certificate out of Peter's hands.)* Okay. I have something to say here.

JULIANA. HEY! !

MARVIN. GIVE that—!

WALTER. Now, now, now I'm not going to set it on fire or anything, just calm down. I just want to say something, and then you can go all go about screwing up each others' lives or whatever. Okay? *(To Peter.)* This isn't to you; go make your phone call.

(PETER leaves. HE will re-enter during the course of this monologue.)

WALTER. What I want to tell you is this: I saw on Donahue last week these five couples all of whom stay together despite the fact that the guy knocks the shit out of the woman on a daily basis. The women were there on the stage, too, toothless wonders all of them. They stayed with these guys because they know deep down that the men really love them. And besides, they didn't get hit unless they did something REALLY wrong. Like *breathe* wrong or, *I* don't know, drop *a plate* or something.

And you know what? You know *what?* I'm
beginning to think that THEY'RE sane and that
YOU people are the crazies! You've GOT to be
crazy! Here these people are battling it out on a
daily basis and you don't want to marry her
because she makes things out of WIRE?? DEAL
WITH IT! This is such a drawback? This is
enough to make you say, "No"? "There's a more
perfect woman out there, just like her except she
doesn't use wire as a medium." "In a perfect
world, my wife uses—" What? "—pastels?" In *this*
world? In *today's* world you're shooting for
perfection? No. Sorr-ree, pal, it's not going to
happen. Because you'll only find something
wrong with the perfect match, too. Because to
accept someone for good is to admit out loud that
you are not strong enough to handle things alone,
that you need someone to accompany you. And
what is wrong with this? NOTHING is. I think it
happens every day. But we get all scared and we
say, "*I* can be alone, *I* am just as happy then as
now." We lie to ourselves all the time. You guys
have something everybody wants, my dumb-ass
friend there, everyone I know. Me. Everybody on
the goddamn planet wants what you have and
you're backing off from it out of fear. And don't
give me these excuses about other people because
it's fear, I know. If you THINK you're happy, you
probably are, don't shoot for the moon. I mean, I
mean—You wanna dump this guy because of a
POLICE SCANNER? (And, my brother has a
police scanner, it's the most annoying device in

this galaxy, squawking like that, BUT DO I
DISOWN MY BROTHER? Go out and get a dog
instead? NO!) What kind of ... do you see what
I'm—... *Stay* with each other. If it wasn't going to
work, you would have known in the course of the
goddamn quarter-century you've already *spent*
with each other. *(Pause. Wired.)* Have I made
myself *clear*??

MARVIN. Yessir.

JULIANA. Yes, you have.

WALTER. Well. *(Pause.)* Good. Umm, here's
your certificate. Do with it what you will.

MARVIN. Thank you.

JULIANA. Thank you.

(Pause.)

MARVIN. Juliana ...?

JULIANA. I know.

MARVIN. Maybe we can try it for a little
while, you know? Maybe we weren't being rash
about getting married. Maybe?

JULIANA. Maybe.

WALTER. *(To Peter.)* What happened.

PETER. She was home. She's coming here.

WALTER. Why did she—

PETER. She said she'd explain when she got
here. That was quite a speech.

WALTER. Oh. Well. Yeah. I mean, it pisses
me off, good nice people being miserable and
stupid toothless people being happy.

PETER. Of course, you don't have a brother.

WALTER. Well, hey, I think we can let the ends justify the means for a change. Huh?

PETER. Fine. That's okay.

WALTER. Just pisses me off.

MARVIN. *(To Walter.)* Ummm ... okay. We're going to, uh. I think we're going to try a little harder.

WALTER. I mean, I mean ... *(Pause.)* Seventy-two hours at *least.*

MARVIN. Thank you for your advice.

WALTER. Hey.

JULIANA. Thank you. *(To Marie.)* Thank you, too. We're sorry.

MARIE. No, no no. Don't worry about it. I'm glad you got it all straightened out.

MARVIN. Oh, we don't have it straightened out. *(Pause. Brightly.)* Thanks again.

(MARVIN and JULIANA exit. MARIE looks after them.)

MARIE. *Oh* yeah, I get a ... I get a *warm glow* whenever I get people like you guys all together. You're planning divorce before you're even *married,* these people here have no CLUE what's ahead of them, they may wind up divorced before they reach the city limits. Or dead. Or something. I'll tell you. I'll tell you. My husband married one hundred people a day in our peak. A *day.* Now my business seems to be putting together people who don't even want to be together. Like I'm MAKING

them get married. Like I sold them something.
You know?

WALTER. Where *is* your husband?

(Pause.)

MARIE. Ohh, well, he felt this sudden urge to
move back to Texas with no particular warning.
That's a while ago now, though.

WALTER. Oh.

MARIE. And I see people just like him come in
and get married every day, and I say to myself
"You're gonna run off, aintcha. Three years,
tops." All while I'm doing the vows. But I just
know it when I see it and I see it all the time.

(Pause.)

PETER. You'd think getting married by
someone who herself is divorced is some kind of
ethical violation.

MARIE. In Las Vegas?

WALTER. Oh yeah, you'd be my choice for the
Ethics Committee Chairperson.

(MISTY enters.)

PETER. THERE you are!

MISTY. Hi ...

PETER. What the hell happened to you?

MISTY. I'm sorry. I left. It was wrong.
Leaving like that.

PETER. Why did you? Weren't we ... didn't we have a nice time ...?

MISTY. Oh yes! It was the most fun I've had in ... I don't even *know*.

PETER. Then why did you leave ...?

MISTY. I just got so ... I got so— *(Pause. To Walter.)* You know what you said to me yesterday?

WALTER. *(Surprised.)* What *I* said to you? What'd I say to you?

MISTY. About flushing my brain down a toilet?

WALTER. Oh. Um. That rings a distant bell.

PETER. You told her to flush her brain down a toilet?

WALTER. Is that what I said?

MISTY. You told me I already had.

WALTER. That's right. *(To Peter.)* I told her she already had.

PETER. Either *way*!

MISTY. No! No, it was right, it was true. I want you to know, I was thinking about it all night. That's why I told you all the things I told you, Peter.

(Pause.)

PETER. Umm. What things were those?

MISTY. Back at your hotel. I know, I know, I wouldn't shut up.

PETER. Back at the ... we had a few drinks and you were talking about ... God. God?

MISTY. Godfrey.

PETER. Godfrey. Not God. Godfrey. *(HE is about to ask who the heck Godfrey is.)*

MISTY. And I knew you wanted to make love, but I had to get it all out of my system.

PETER. Wh—wait, wait—

MISTY. And you were such a good listener, I felt so *human* again talking to you—

PETER. We didn't—uh. We didn't have ...?

MISTY. No, and I'm sorry. I *am* sorry.

PETER. We didn't—wait, remind me who Godf—

MISTY. Because I've been here so long, and nobody ever cares what I say, just as long as I serve the drinks. It was so nice of you to hear me last night. That's why I'm sorry, because it would have been making love, it wouldn't have been sex, you see? There was that extra *attachment* ... But then I guess we fell asleep.

PETER. You felt an attachment?

MISTY. Yes. Because not everyone would have listened. Others would say "You wanna finish this story quick and get under the covers?"

(Pause.)

PETER. I'm going to feel awful if I don't say this ...

MISTY. What?

PETER. I mean, I'm really sorry, but, ummm ... All the things I listened so intently to last night, I don't remember a damn thing about them. I have no clue on earth who Godfrey is.

MISTY. That's okay. You were drunk. You still listened, though. And I got so scared laying there—

PETER. Wait, wait, you don't understand. I was also hinting that I'd LIKE TO KNOW who Godfrey is. Remind me.

MISTY. Oh. Oh. Godfrey was an ex-boyfriend of mine who said that I'd never make it as a dancer because I was too stupid to manage myself and not talented enough to get an agent.

PETER. Oh.

MISTY. He also said I had a smile like a jack-o'-lantern carved by a drunk.

PETER. Great guy, this guy.

MISTY. That was when I broke up to come out here. He threw a jar at me. And he's been just typical. You have no idea. (*To Walter.*) And here I actually DEFEND myself when you say I've thrown my brain down the toilet—you're right! I do it every time I go out with one of those assholes. And I was doing it last night, too.

PETER. Thanks a lot.

MISTY. I mean, I mean, you were just going to go away. We were just going to get up in the morning and get divorced and go away. I didn't want to do that, but I didn't know what to do. So I just left. I'm sorry. I was drunk at the time, I didn't know what to do.

PETER. Okay. I'm ... I'm glad you got to tell me. I really am.

MISTY. *Are* you?

PETER. Yes. Yes. Really.

MISTY. I'm, really, I'm relieved.

PETER. No, no, it's fine.

MISTY. Guys get so scared off when a girl— well, maybe not any girl, but *me*—when "attachment" is used.

PETER. You hate it here.

MISTY. Las Vegas? God, yes. I'm going to start getting my act togeth—

PETER. Fine, then, come back to New York with us.

MISTY. What?

WALTER. WAIT WAIT *WAIT* WAIT WAIT wait wait.

PETER. I know what I'm doing.

WALTER. Yeah? What, then?

PETER. I'm a married man. We're going to get divorced. We were *going* to get divorced today, so what the hell does it matter if we wait a week or so. We could just as easily get divorced in New York. What the hell. She wants to leave anyway. Right?

MISTY. Do you mean this??

PETER. Yeah. Yeah. Why not?

WALTER. Why *not*? Why NOT? *I'll* tell you why not. You know her twenty-four hours! You're too lazy to get divorced to this total stranger today, so instead you're going to put her in your suitcase like a souvenir??

PETER. Walter.

WALTER. What??

PETER. If you'll think for a minute—

WALTER. If *I'll* think? *I'll* tell you who has to think—

PETER. Hey, who'd you just give advice to? A couple that's known each other thirteen years and still can't decide to be happy.

WALTER. Look what you're doing—!

PETER. I know what I'm doing!

WALTER. She says the magic word, "attachment," and BLAMMO, you're attached.

PETER. Yeah, not like you, you hear that word and you jump out a seventh-story window. Well, screw it. What am I waiting for? We have what everyone wants. And if we lose it, if it doesn't work, we'll just go back to plan A and get divorced. Join the fifty percent divorce rate. What the hell.

WALTER. This isn't what everybody wants. I was talking about a normal relationship. THAT'S what everybody wants. This is not normal. You see?

PETER. Who has normal? Who the hell has normal? Since no one I *know* actually has normal, I'm just gonna make do. You know? *(To Marie.)* I'm going to ask you to renew our vows.

MARIE. You got married last night. People usually wait twenty-five years.

PETER. I don't have twenty-five years. I still have plenty of money left.

MARIE. No, that's fine. That's fine.

PETER. No, look, I—

MARIE. No, no. *(Pause.)* On me. I think you paid enough.

MISTY. Peter—?

PETER. Yeah.

MISTY. We did this really impulsively last night and now we're doing it again. Are you sure?

PETER. Yeah. *(Pause.)* No. I'm not sure.

MISTY. I've never been to New York City.

PETER. Do you want to do this?

(Pause.)

MISTY. Yeah.

PETER. Are you sure?

(Pause.)

MISTY. No.

PETER. Perfect. Let's get this going. *(To Walter.)* I'm going to ask you to be our witness.

WALTER. You know I only jump down your throat when you're doing something dumb.

PETER. I know. Please be my witness now.

WALTER. I think this is dumb.

PETER. Me too.

WALTER. Well, as long as we agree. *(To Marie.)* Okay, you can start now.

PETER. Thank you.

WALTER. I'm glad for you. *(Pause.)* I hope this is a good thing.

MARIE. I guess I'll just do the same as last night. Here we are. *(Pause.)* We are gathered

here this evening to join Peter Gatesman and
Misty Sunday Merriwether, two—

MISTY. Gladys Kravitz!

MARIE. What?

MISTY. That's my real name. Gladys
Kravitz.

MARIE. Okay, hon. Peter Gatesman and
Gladys Kravitz, two people who wish to express
and bind their love together in front of these good
people and the state of Nevada.

*(The ceremony continues in silence as MUSIC
swells up. PETER kisses the bride. The
LIGHTS fade.)*

End of Play

Other Publications For Your Interest

SIS BOOM BAA. Comedy. Sybil Rosen. 2m., 4f. Int. Football widows of America: This Is Your Life! Pam, Cheryl, Linda and Mary are best friends. They do everything together—because their husbands spend most of their time watching football on TV. Says Pam: "Compulsive football-watching is a male-reaction formation to the stress of being civilized. It's more bonding than Crazy Glue." Mary, the new-comer to the group has recently married Joey, and his obsession is really getting to her. While the women cook New Year's Day dinner in Cheryl's kitchen they coach Mary on technique—on how to get Joey's attention away from the game. We finally meet Joey when he comes into the kitchen for something to eat; and Mary tries what she has learned on him, to no avail—so she tackles him! **(#21681)**

FREEZE TAG. Comedy. Jacquelyn Reingold. 2f Ext. When Andrea tries to buy a newspaper in NYC's East Village, she is thrust onto an emotional journey she will never forget. Aldrich, the newsstand vendor, seems to know the most intimate secrets of Andrea's life, from childhood up to the present moment, including who her boyfriend is sleeping with and why. In this funny and touching play, two women are forced to confront who they are, who they once were, and what it means to be a friend. "Gripping and hilarious."—N.Y. Times. "Really terrific . . . one of the most impressive [playwriting] debuts of the season."—N.Y. Press. "An extraordinary play . . . an unforgettable experience."—Back Stage. **(#8678)**

LOOKIN' FOR A BETTER BERRY BUSH. Comic Drama. Jean Lenox Toddie (author of *Tell Me Another Story Sing Me a Song*, *A Scent of Honeysuckle* and *A Bag of Green Apples*). 2f. Ext. (simply suggested). Emma and Addie confront each other on the sidewalk of a city neighborhood. Emma is a proper woman who worked in a diner for forty years and "served more cups of coffee than you can count if you live to be a hundred." Addie, a street woman whose papa "set us t' wanderin' jes' a-lookin' fer a better berry bush," rummages in trash cans and sleeps in a cardboard box. This is the humorous and touching tale of two women, alienated from each other by vastly different life experience, who clash on a city street, only to find themselves sitting down together on a stoop in front of a brownstone, and tentatively reaching out for mutual understanding. **(#14927)**

Penguin Blues

by Ethan Phillips

Comic Drama. 1m., 1f. Int. This beautiful short play by actor Ethan Phillips of TV's "Benson" wowed them at Philadelphia Festival Theatre for New Plays. The critics were unanimous in their praise. We are in a room in an alcoholism rehabilitation center. The characters are Gordon, a manic alcoholic who knows the score, and Angelica, a nun who denies that she is an alcoholic. In the moving climax, Angelica finally recognizes why she is there; and in so doing, takes the painful first step towards sobriety. "One of the loveliest moments of emotional revelation I've seen in the theatre."—News of Delaware County.

(#18934)

Portfolio

by Tom Donaghy

Comedy. 1m., 1f., plus 1 offstage voice. Int. This amusing satire of advertising was produced to great audience mirth and critical approval at NYC's famed comedy theatre, Manhattan Punchline. We are on a photo shoot for a print ad campaign. The photographer, who is present only by voice, has had the brilliant idea to deck his model with live pigeons. He's hired a "pigeon man" to bring in a truckload of them. He becomes most annoyed, though, when the pigeons (which are mimed, by the way), won't take direction as easily as the model, much to the distress of the hapless pigeon man. Meanwhile, the model remains unflappable. In her business, she's used to anything and everything! (#18952)

Haiku

by Katherine Snodgrass

Drama. 3f., Int. This sublimely beautiful short play won the prestigious Heidemann Award given by the Actors Theatre of Louisville, perhaps the most important one-act play award in the United States. The story concerns a woman who lives with her retarded daughter, who has miraculously at brief intervals been "normal." In fact, the daughter, Louise, is sometimes super-normal, speaking in beautiful haiku poetry, which her mother has recorded and has had published under the mother's name. Then an older daughter, Billie, comes for a visit. Billie only knows her sister as hopelessly retarded, and refuses to believe that her mother's poetry has actually been composed by her sister. (#10650)

INCIDENT AT SAN BAJO
Drama
by Brad Korbesmeyer

3m., 4f. Bare Stage. The residents of a trailer camp at San Bajo have quite a story to tell, about a stranger who visited each one in turn, selling a mysterious elixir which he claimed would make them "live longer." Most of the residents of San Bajo did not buy the elixir of course—and they are now dead, the water supply having been poisoned by the mysterious stranger. Only seven are left to tell the tale—the seven who drank the elixir which, it turned out, was an antidote! Each tells his story in a series of interlocking monologues given to an unseen interviewer. The effect is somewhat like a "60 Minutes" segment, with an imaginary Morley Safer. This most unusual new play was the 1988 winner of Actors Theatre of Louisville's Heidemann Award, perhaps the most prestigious one-act play award in the United States. (#11654)

BAIT AND SWITCH
Comedy
by Richard Dresser

3m., 2f. Int. Doug and Gary own and run a restaurant on the boardwalk which is fast going under, largely due to a recent influx of stinging jellyfish which has kept customers away from the beach, but also due to the fact that the two brothers are less than adept businessmen—particularly Gary, who isn't even aware that his brother is skimming profits. Their only hope is Kenny, a slick wiseguy with possible Mob connections. Kenny meets with Gary and Doug, sizes up the situation immediately, and eventually does take over the restaurant, forcing the two brothers out and, possibly, ending up with Gary's wife Lucy as part of the deal. Another incisive comic look at the American entrepreneurial mentality from the author of *The Downside, Better Days* and *Alone at the Beach*. (#3948)

TONE CLUSTERS
Joyce Carol Oates
Drama

1m., 1f., plus 1 male voice. Bare stage. Frank and Emily Gulick are a nice middle-American couple with a nice house in a nice neighborhood. Why, then are they obviously under so much strain? As they are interviewed by an unseen interrogator, their story, and their predicament, emerges. The mutilated body of a 14 year-old girl from the neighborhood has been found in their basement, and their son is charged with the murder. Desperately, they cling to the belief that their son is not guilty, even as it becomes increasingly clear that he is the murderer. And, even as we are moved by the pitiable Gulicks, we ask ourselves, do they somehow share in the guilt of the crime? And: could we, as parents, someday find ourselves in their predicament? This extraordinary play by one of America's foremost women of letters won the prestigious Heideman Award bestowed by Actors Theatre of Louisville, which commissioned it and gave it its world premier at the famed Humana Festival. In *In Darkest America*.   (#22727)

THE ECLIPSE
Joyce Carol Oates
Drama

1m., 3f Int. Stephanie Washburn, a middle-aged college professor, lives with her mother Muriel in a small apartment in Philadelphia. Muriel was once a brilliant high school teacher. Now, she is retired, and her mind is going, possibly from Alzheimer's disease. As she goes in and out of reality, she makes her daughter's life miserable, even going so far as to call the local department of social services to accuse Stephanie of abusing her—a total fabrication, of course. Muriel also has a fantasy that she has a Latin lover, a Señor Rios, with whom she is carrying on a torrid affair. There is no Señor Rios, of course. Or is there? In the end, as flamenco music plays, Muriel enters, in a Spanish dancing dress, for her big date with Señor Rios, who appears, exactly as Muriel has described him, for a torrid dance with Muriel around the apartment as Stephanie sleeps in a chair, oblivious to it all. Then Muriel leaves for her date with the dark gentleman, and both women are finally released from their suffering. Death has finally claimed Muriel. This haunting play by one of America's foremost women of letters was commissioned by the Actors Theatre of Louisville, which produced it as part of their famed Humana Festival, and was subsequently produced Off Broadway in New York by Ensemble Studio Theatre. In *In Darkest America*.   (#7633)

STEAK NIGHT

Comedy
by Richard Polak

3m. 2f. Int. This is an amusing yet somewhat chilling look at an American family which is doing something about the so-called decline in family values. The family has a strict set of rules, and if you break one the other family members get to vote on the nature, length and severity of your punishment. The voting always takes place on the night the family has steak for dinner—sort of a family tradition, you might say. The most enthusiastic participant in this rite is Alan, a somewhat bullying 16-year-old; until, that is, he transgresses and the family votes on his punishment! Very cleverly, very deviously, Alan swings the vote in his favor and, in fact, takes over the family! "A dark little comedy with deepening layers ... provides a metaphor, both telling and chilling, of the ease with which a really determined, clever leader can and does use democracy to overthrow democracy ... playwright Polak combines grim Kafkaesque elements with a natural American embullience."—Drama-Logue. (#21342)

TOTALLY COOL

Drama
by Jan Buttram

2m., 2f, to play 6m. 2f. Unit set. This terrific new drama depicts the relationship between two seemingly average teenage girls, Connie and Suzy, and shows how the two descend into destructive substance abuse. The play dramatizes both the emotional and physical consequences inherent in drug use. Both funny and sad, at times lighthearted and intense, *Totally Cool* mixes extreme realism and dream-like qualities to create a stirring and thought provoking experience. The dramatic landscape includes a variety of characters who help complete the story of Connie and Suzy; two paramedics, a pair of morgue attendants and the local medical examiner and his sidekick. (#22724)

TWO NEW COMEDIES FROM
SAMUEL FRENCH, Inc.

FAST GIRLS. (Little Theatre). Comedy. Diana Amsterdam. 2m., 3f. Int. Lucy Lewis is a contemporary, single woman in her thirties with what used to be called a "healthy sex life," much to the chagrin of her mother, who feels Lucy is too fast, too easy—and too single. Her best friend, on the other hand, neighbor Abigail McBride, is deeply envious of Lucy's ease with men. When Lucy wants to date a man she just calls him up, whereas Abigail sits home alone waiting for Ernest, who may not even know she exists, to call. The only time Abigail isn't by the phone is after Lucy has had a hot date, when she comes over to Lucy's apartment to hear the juicy details and get green with envy. Sometimes, though, Lucy doesn't want to talk about it, which drives Abigail *nuts* ("If you don't tell me about men I have no love life!"). Lucy's mother arrives to take the bull by the horns, so to speak, arriving with a challenge. Mom claims no man will marry Lucy (even were she to *want to* get married), because she's too easy. Lucy takes up the challenge, announcing that she is going to get stalwart ex-boyfriend Sidney ("we're just friends") Epstein to propose to her. Easier said than done. Sidney doesn't *want* a fast girl. Maybe dear old Mom is right, thinks Lucy. Maybe fast girls *can't* have it all. "Amsterdam makes us laugh, listen and think."—Daily Record. "Brilliantly comic moments."—The Monitor. "rapidly paced comedy with a load of laughs . . . a funny entertainment with some pause for reflection on today's [sexual] confusion."—Suburban News. "Takes a penetrating look at [contemporary sexual chaos]. Passion, celibacy, marriage, fidelity are just some of the subjects that Diana Amsterdam hilariously examines."—Tribune News.   (#8149)

ADVICE FROM A CATERPILLAR. (Little Theatre.) Comedy. Douglas Carter Beane. 2m. 2f. 1 Unit set & 1 Int. Ally Sheedy and Dennis Christopher starred in the delightful off-Broadway production of this hip new comedy. Ms. Sheedy played Missy, an avant garde video artist who specializes in re-runs of her family's home videos, adding her own disparaging remarks. Needless to say, she is very alienated from the middle-class, family values she grew up with, which makes her very *au courant*, but strangely unhappy. She has a successful career and a satisfactory love-life with a businessman named Suit. Suit's married, but that doesn't stop him and Missy from carrying on. Something's missing, though—and Missy isn't sure what it is, until she meets Brat. He is a handsome young aspiring actor. Unfortunately, Brat is also the boyfriend of Missy's best friend. Sound familiar? It isn't—because Missy's best friend is a gay man named Spaz! Spaz has been urging Missy to find an unmarried boyfriend, but this is too much—too much for Spaz, too much for Suit and, possibly, too much for Missy. Does she *want* a serious relationship (ugh—how bourgeois!)? Can a bisexual unemployed actor actually be her Mr. Wonderful? "Very funny ... a delightful evening."—Town & Village.   (#3876)

Other Publications for Your Interest

MOVIE OF THE MONTH
(COMEDY)

By DANIEL MELTZER

2 men—Interior

This new comedy by the author of the ever-popular *The Square Root of Love* is an amusing satire of commercial television. B.S., a TV programming executive, is anxious to bolster his network's ratings, which have been sagging of late due to programming disasters such as a documentary called "The Ugly Truth" (says B.S.: "What the hell is The Ugly Truth, and how the hell did it get into our Prime Time?") His eagerbeaver assistant, appropriately named Broun, has found a script which he is sure can be made into a hit "Movie of the Month". It's about this Danish prince, see, who comes home from college to find that his uncle has murdered his father and married his mother . . . Well, naturally, B.S. has his own ideas about how to fix such a totally unbelievable plot . . .   (#17621)

SUNDANCE
(ALL GROUPS—COMEDY)

By MEIR Z. RIBALOW

5 men—Simple interior

This new comedy from the author of *Shrunken Heads* is set in a sort of metaphysical wild west saloon. The characters include Hickock, Jesse, the Kid, and the inevitable Barkeep. Hickock kills to uphold the law. Jesse kills for pleasure. The Kid kills to bring down The Establishment. What if, wonders the Barkeep, they met up with the Ultimate Killer—who kills for no reason, who kills simply because that's what he does? Enter Sundance. He does not kill to uphold the law, for pleasure, or to make a political statement, or because he had a deprived childhood. And he proceeds to kill everyone, exiting at the end with his sixguns blazing! "Witty, strong, precise, unusually well-written."—The Guardian. "A brilliant piece."—Dublin Evening Press. This co-winner of the 1981 Annual NYC Metropolitan Short Play Festival has been a success in 6 countries!   (#3113)